Italian Greyhound Guide

Italian Greyhound Guide Includes: Italian Greyhound Training, Diet, Socializing, Care, Grooming, Breeding and More

---

Connor Bailey

ISBN 978-1-5269-0731-8

My Thanks To...

I would like to start by thanking the many wonderful Italian Greyhound breeders in existence today. Through your hard work and dedication, we are fortunate enough to experience the many joys that come with owning and training this great breed.

Thank you to my publishers that have allowed for this book to become a reality.

A Big Thank You to my family for their loving support during this project.

Table of Contents

Introduction & Foreword

"He is your friend, your partner, your defender, your dog.

You are his life, his love, his leader.

He will be yours, faithful and true, to the last beat of his heart.

You owe it to him to be worthy of such devotion."

Congratulations on your decision to embark on the journey of Italian Greyhound ownership. Perhaps you are thinking about a future in breeding Italian Greyhounds. Or perhaps your interest is simply in having a loyal family pet. Either way, owning an Italian Greyhound will provide you with years of enjoyment and companionship.

Investing in an Italian Greyhound and making it part of your family is also a significant commitment. It is wise to learn all you can about caring for the new addition.

Our aim and hope is that you take away a series of useful tips and advice after reading this book. Our intention is for you to benefit in some way, and we're confident that you will.

Enjoy growing a loving bond with your Italian Greyhound.

Chapter One: Finding a Healthy Italian Greyhound

Finding a healthy Italian Greyhound puppy for sale can be challenging. If you do not find an Italian Greyhound puppy for sale immediately, or you do not find a breeder you like, keep checking with different breeders and maintain communication. Even if a breeder does not currently have a litter, they could be planning a litter in the next few months. Build a relationship with a reputable breeder who will advise you about upcoming litters. It is not unusual to be put on a waiting list for a pedigreed puppy.

It is always important to build relationships with breeders, not just to obtain information about their puppies, but to discover if they are trustworthy.

If you ever feel uncomfortable with a breeder, choose a different one. Trust your gut instinct and do not settle. Remember that this is an animal that you will be spending 12 to 15 years with so starting with the right breeder will ensure you have the right dog.

Finding a Reputable Breeder

We have all heard stories of backyard breeders and "puppy mills" where dogs live in sub-standard conditions and are bred indiscriminately, with no care for the resulting health or well-being of their puppies. How can you know if a breeder is reputable? There are some basic qualifications you can use, even before visiting a kennel, to learn if a relationship with a breeder is worth pursuing.

A breeder that will answer questions

While most breeders have full time jobs and family commitments in addition to their breeding business, a good Italian Greyhound breeder should always be happy to answer your questions. The breeder should be open to discussing the breed with you and potential puppy ownership. Be wary of breeders whose first concern is obtaining your deposit to hold a future puppy.

Ask if the breeder requires a home check. You may find that many breeders are initially distrusting of you. This is actually a good sign, as it shows they are concerned that you intend to provide your Italian Greyhound puppy with a good home environment.

A breeder that is active with the breed club and kennel club

Ask a breeder what breed club or kennel club their puppies are registered with. You can also ask if their puppies show and how they place.

Ask if both of the parents of the puppy you are offered are registered with a breed or kennel club. If one of the parents is not registered, you will not be able to register the puppy. This is especially important if you intend to allow your Italian Greyhound puppy to be bred in the future.

A breeder that can give you backgrounds on their Italian Greyhounds

Choose a breeder that knows the background of their Italian Greyhounds such as pedigree, health of the lines and where the Italian Greyhounds came from. The breeder should also know the history of the breed and the breed standard.

A breeder that has a puppy plan and health clearances

Look for a breeder that has a breeding plan for their overall kennel.

Are they trying to breed a certain temperament or feature of the dogs or just breeding to produce puppies? Do they have a breeding plan (a goal in mind as to how to further the health and integrity of the breed)? Do they have a plan for how the puppies should be raised? Can they talk to you knowledgeably about socialization and temperament?

A good breeder should also be able to provide proof of health clearances on all their dogs and should welcome questions about the dogs' good health. These include:

1. Eyes Certified

2. Factor VII Status

3. OFA Thyroid

4. OFA Cardiac

5. OFA Knees

A breeder that has good references

Finally, make sure that the breeder has excellent references. References can come from vets, contacts who have previously bought puppies, and contacts from other breeders.

Asking about price

Breeders invest much into a litter and may not welcome your inquiries if your first or only question is about price. Spend some time talking to the breeder about their dogs first. Demonstrate your seriousness and commitment as an owner. Show that you care about more than just price. Once you have established rapport with the breeder and have made inquiries about health of their Italian Greyhounds or the breeding program, you can make inquiries about the price of a puppy from the next litter.

Suggested Breeder Interview Questions

Below is a list of helpful questions you can ask a breeder, whether speaking in person or over the telephone:

1) How long have you been breeding?

2) Are you an affiliated breeder of The Kennel Club/American Kennel Club or any other Italian Greyhound club?

3) When was the last time your premises were inspected by an official from the Kennel Club?

4) What are the breed standard characteristics?

5) What is the standard Italian Greyhound temperament?

6) What are the main health problems for this breed?

7) Do you carry out health screenings on breeding pairs before breeding a litter?

8) Can you give me a copy of the bloodline breeding documents and a full set of health-screening certificates?

9) How much exercise does an Italian Greyhound need as a puppy and as an adult?

10) Do your Italian Greyhounds bark a lot?

11) How often does an Italian Greyhound need to be groomed?

12) What are the best training methods for an Italian Greyhound puppy?

13) At what age does puberty usually begin?

14) How long before s/he acts like an adult dog?

15) Is this breed safe with young children?

16) Does this breed get along well with other pets?

17) Will there be any "endorsements" on the Contract of Sale?

18) Do you have an overall breeding plan?

19) Do you show your dogs at The Kennel Club/AKC events?

Visiting the Breeder

Once you are confident you have located a good breeder with a solid reputation, it is time to schedule a visit to their kennel. Note that if the breeder has a recent litter, they may not allow a visit. This is a step that responsible breeders take in order to ensure the puppies remain healthy and free from infection while they are very young (less than four or five weeks).

At any other time, the breeder should welcome a visit. Here are some important things you can do on your visit.

Check to see that puppies are raised indoors

While Italian Greyhounds do enjoy time outside, it is important for the socialization and health of all puppies to be raised in the home.

Italian Greyhounds that live indoors, recognizing a human as the authoritative figure, will be more or less home-trained and accustomed to people and other dogs.

Early socialization by a good breeder can save you a lot of training time and challenges later.

Inspecting the kennel

Check the hygiene standards of the breeder's kennels, as good breeders will have a clean environment for their adult and puppy Italian Greyhounds. Puppies that come from a dirty, poorly managed kennel can have many health and behavioral problems.

Observe how the breeder and Italian Greyhounds behave around each other. If the Italian Greyhounds show any signs of being wary or cringing away from the breeder, this is a sign of poor treatment that will almost certainly result in behavior problems in the puppies.

If the kennel has a litter that can be viewed, take a look at the puppies with their mother, to observe the behavior of both. Good Italian Greyhound breeders will always be happy to allow this, as they are keen to get to know you and see how you interact with their much-loved Italian Greyhound pups. Respectable sellers will want to check that you are going to be a responsible dog owner, able to provide the best care and training to one of their carefully bred puppies.

Healthy Italian Greyhounds

Remember that nursing mothers will look a little 'frayed around the edges', especially if they are nursing a large litter. Nursing mothers tend to lose weight and their coat thins after they produce a litter and feed several hungry puppies.

However, the rest of the dogs should look healthy and have good levels of energy. It is important to look at all of the dogs, not just the parents of the puppies, to see how they are maintained by the breeder. If any dog looks unwell, question the breeder about it.

Ask to see pedigree documents

Reputable breeders will always have the necessary paperwork ready to show purchasers. This includes a record of the puppy's bloodline or, in the case of a rescue Italian Greyhound, the name and phone number of the previous owner.

If you buy from any who cannot provide the official paperwork, you will be taking a serious financial risk and potentially encouraging the cruel treatment of Italian Greyhounds and dogs in general.

Ask to see health certificates

Breeders should have copies of health certificates proving the puppy has been tested for diseases that the Italian Greyhound may be prone to.

What the breeder expects of you

Remember that the breeder is interviewing you too. You can expect a breeder to ask you questions and to look into your references. Dog breeders put a lot of time, effort, and money, not to mention their love for their dogs, into breeding a litter of puppies. It can take years to plan a breeding and produce a litter. Breeders are often very choosy about their clientele. If the breeder feels uncomfortable with you, they do have the right to refuse to sell you a puppy.

Your job is to convince the breeder that you will provide a wonderful home for one of their puppies. The breeder may have a questionnaire for you. They may want to visit your home and talk to your veterinary references. Be prepared to talk to the breeder and answer some questions.

Whether in person or via telephone or email, refer to the rule of thumb explained above when it comes to asking about price.

Choosing your Italian Greyhound

Once you have selected the breeder and the litter is born, it is time to select your puppy. In most cases the breeder will help determine which puppy is a good match for you. Breeders usually have years of experience and can determine a puppy's temperament. They are good at matching puppies with people.

Sometimes a breeder will give you the choice of two or three puppies. Be open about gender and color. It will help the breeder know which puppies might suit you.

If you are looking for a show puppy, choose one that has the looks and temperament of the breed standard. If you are looking for a pet, you can choose any color and do not need to be as concerned about the breed standard.

After the selections have been narrowed down between pet and show quality puppies, you can begin your choice. Take the time to watch the puppies as they play together. Look for a puppy with an even temperament. Do not believe the myth that the puppy will choose you. Often, the puppy that runs up and greets you is the most outgoing in the litter. While that is not always a bad thing, if you are looking for a quieter puppy, the outgoing one is not the best match. Similarly, do not choose the shy puppy or one that hides. A shy puppy may grow up to have some temperament problems later in life.

Instead, look for a puppy that looks around, assesses the situation and then comes to you. This is usually the sign of a middle-of-the-road temperament. A puppy that behaves in this way is neither too reserved or fearful, nor too outgoing or pushy.

In addition to looking at temperament, look at the health of your puppy. You want to choose a puppy with the following traits:

Alert and energetic: Avoid a puppy that seems lethargic. If you arrive during puppy nap time, wait until the Italian Greyhound puppies are awake.

Bright Eyes: Eyes should be clear of any debris and should not have any discharge. The Italian Greyhound should have bright, shiny eyes. These will often have a blue tone for puppies under 6 weeks of age.

Excellent Body Condition: Look at the overall condition of the body and coat. The coat should be rich and soft without crusty areas, dandruff, or dullness. The overall body of the puppy should be fat enough that the ribs are not easily discernible on sight, but thin enough that they can be felt when you touch its sides.

Nose: The puppy's nose should be shiny and wet. In addition, the puppy should have no problems breathing.

Excellent Sight and Hearing: Clap your hands or encourage the puppy to chase toys. Watch its reaction. If you see any signs that it cannot hear or see, you may want to choose a different puppy. Although you will be focused on your main choice of Italian Greyhound puppy, it is important to watch all of the puppies. If you notice signs of disease, choose a different breeder or litter.

Puppies should not mind being touched or handled. If the puppy struggles or becomes fearful, you may want to discuss a different pick with your breeder. Taking your time with the puppies and visiting them more than once will help you choose the right one. Remember to take advantage of the input of the breeder and be sure to follow your own instincts as well.

In the end, this will be a relationship that lasts a very long time, so make sure it is the right one for you and your Italian Greyhound puppy from the start.

Completing the Sale

When you are fully satisfied that you have found a good breeder and a healthy puppy, you are ready to purchase. Before you take your puppy home, however, ensure you receive all the important paperwork related to your puppy and the sale.

1) A Contract of Sale clearly shows the responsibilities to the puppy of both the Breeder and the Buyer.

The contract should also list any official Kennel Club endorsements (or restrictions) that the breeder has placed on the puppy's records. For example, a breeder may specify that a puppy is "not for breeding" if there is a high risk of passing on a genetic medical condition. Even though the puppy may not be suffering from the condition, it could be a carrier of a disease or other medical condition. Alternatively, the breeder may note that an older Italian Greyhound female is past the age of breeding. A breeder may also note that an Italian Greyhound is "not for export."

It should be clearly stated under what conditions the breeder may be prepared to remove the endorsement. You must give a signed acknowledgement of any endorsement placed on the Contract of Sale, either before or at the time the sale is officially completed.

Every good breeder should be utterly committed that none of their dogs end up in rescue. Therefore their contract should have a clause that says the Italian Greyhound has a permanent home with the owner. It should also have a clause that says the breeder can repossess the Italian Greyhound if there is significant evidence of abuse or neglect.

2) Written advice on training, feeding, exercise, worming and immunization.

3) A pedigree document detailing the dog's ancestry. This could be hand-written or a printed pedigree from the breeder or an official one from the kennel club.

4) Registration materials.

5) A record of which vaccinations your puppy has received and which ones are still required.

6) Copies of any additional health certificates for both the dog and the bitch. There are also some DNA tests now available for certain breeds. Ask if these are available.

7) Insurance certificate. The breeder should offer you 4 weeks free Kennel Club/AKC Pet Insurance for your new puppy, which starts from the moment you collect your puppy. Check this has actually been set up and do not leave until you have the Certificate of Insurance in your possession. This cover is important, should your new puppy suffer from any illness or injury before you have time to take out long-term insurance.

8) Some breeders offer a guarantee for their dogs. Check with your breeder and ensure that you clearly understand the terms of the guarantee.

Note: Never complete a sale with a breeder that promises to send the documents to you later.

Adopting an Older Italian Greyhound

Although much of this chapter is focused on finding an Italian Greyhound puppy, it is important to touch on choosing an adult Italian Greyhound. While it is not common, it is possible to find an older Italian Greyhound. This can be a retired Italian Greyhound from a breeding kennel, a rescued Italian Greyhound, or an older Italian Greyhound puppy that the breeder has decided not to keep.

Adopting an older Italian Greyhound has many advantages:

a) Housebroken: Many adult Italian Greyhounds are housebroken when you adopt them so you do not have to house train them.

b) Less destructive: This varies from Italian Greyhound to Italian Greyhound but many are trained before they arrive in your home. This means they are less likely to give in to bad habits such as destructive chewing.

c) Affectionate: Although most Italian Greyhounds are affectionate, many older dogs have an almost grateful demeanor with their new owners.

d) Trainable: The old saying, "You can't teach an old dog new tricks," is actually not true. You can teach cues to older dogs.

It is important to note that it does take time for an older Italian Greyhound to adjust to its new home and it may be withdrawn during that time. In general, it is recommended that you give it about one year to adjust to the change.

Choosing an Italian Greyhound from a Rescue

Choosing an Italian Greyhound from a rescue can be a wonderful way to add to your family while helping a dog in need. Decide ahead if you have time to invest in housebreaking. Do you have children to consider? If so, you will want to find an Italian Greyhound that will not threaten their safety. Is your household sedentary or active? How much time will you have to give your new dog? All of these factors should help you decide on the age and energy level of the Italian Greyhound you bring home.

Decide before visiting the rescue whether you want a puppy, an adolescent dog or a mature dog. A puppy has the potential to be more trainable than an older dog, but will have more energy and require more work in housebreaking and training. Adolescent dogs are full of energy, and will likely be at their worst in the shelter, but can respond well to affection and a new home. Older dogs are already housebroken and have less energy than younger dogs.

Before you leave for the rescue, prepare your mindset. It is easy to let emotions interfere with good judgment when you look for an Italian Greyhound at a rescue. But remember you will live with your decision for years. Make up your mind to resist both pleading canine eyes and the pleas of shelter employees about a dog's fate. Determine to make your decision based on an Italian Greyhound's compatibility with your family's energy level and lifestyle.

Be sure to take the whole family when visiting a rescue. Everyone will need to be happy with the decision, and you will want to assess the Italian Greyhound's reactions to your children.

Some dog rescues use foster homes. The Italian Greyhound's temporary owners may be able to tell you things about the dog, such as whether it gets along well with other animals, what kind of activity level it has and how it socializes with people and other dogs.

Determining Your Potential Italian Greyhound's Temperament

At the shelter, use your time effectively to learn everything you can about the Italian Greyhound. If you are not meeting at a dog's foster home or in a neutral place, but in the shelter itself, recognize that the dogs are in the worst possible situation: a noisy and chaotic environment in which they have been kenneled for long periods of time. The advantage to this situation is that it gives you a revealing look at the dog's character. Note whether it is nervous, defensive, startled or friendly.

Judge whether or not your potential Italian Greyhound is friendly by watching its body language. A friendly dog:

a) wiggles when you approach

b) has an open mouth and squinting eyes

c) wags its tail low, soft and loose

Put your hand near the bars of the kennel, but not inside. Does this Italian Greyhound move close to be stroked? Raise your hand quickly. Does it cower, show aggression or wag its tail? A dog that has been abused will have special issues that need to be overcome and this is a good way to assess whether or not that has been the case. If you have children in your home, you will want to avoid Italian Greyhounds that show aggression.

Try staring at this Italian Greyhound. How does it react? A well socialized dog will understand that human staring is not a sign of aggression, but a signal to approach. Look for a friendly response.

Some simple tests

Try a few simple tests to assess the Italian Greyhound's reactions. Is it curious, nervous, hyper or defensive? How does it respond in the following situations?

a) when called?

b) when offered a treat?

c) if there is a loud noise (try throwing an object such as a tin can)?

d) to human affection and touch?

e) to grooming with a brush?

Find out if you can take the Italian Greyhound on a "test drive," and take it for a walk. Taking it for a walk offers several advantages over seeing it in the shelter. It gives the pooch a chance to work out the anxiety it may have from being kenneled, and you will have a better chance to assess its personality and see it in the context of a good owner-dog bonding activity.

While this Italian Greyhound is on the leash, walk past other dogs. How does it react? Does it appear to be well-socialized with other dogs?

After a walk, try playing with it using a toy or ball. Ask it to sit and tempt it with a treat. Try to assess how easy this Italian Greyhound will be to train. Most intelligent Italian Greyhounds will easily understand how to behave in order to get the treat.

Meeting Existing Pets

Some shelters will allow you to bring along existing dogs to introduce to a potential one. If you plan to introduce the new Italian Greyhound to a dog that you already own, try walking them together first, parallel to one another. Avoid introducing them head to head or in a confined space.

You can't tell everything about an Italian Greyhound in a single meeting at a rescue, but these brief assessments should help you to make the best decision about compatibility with your family and lifestyle.

Chapter Two: Preparing for Your Italian Greyhound Puppy

Bringing a puppy into your home is always exciting, and preparing for the day your puppy officially becomes part of its "forever family" is part of the fun. While every dog owner is different, there are some common supplies that you will want to have on hand for your Italian Greyhound.

It is important to note that the supplies you need for an Italian Greyhound puppy are fairly basic. You do not need to purchase everything your pet store recommends. In this chapter, we will discuss necessary supplies and those that are optional. We will also look at how to puppy-proof your home.

General Supplies

It is not necessary to purchase many things as you prepare for your pup. However, it is important to have a few supplies before you bring your puppy home. Bowls and puppy food, for example, are items that must be purchased ahead of time. And it is not recommended to take your puppy shopping with you before it has had its vaccinations.

Here is a list of essential supplies:

Feeding Bowls

Make sure your puppy can reach its food and water easily. Stainless steel bowls are best, as they are durable and easier to keep hygienic and clean.

Ceramic bowls are also a good choice, provided they are dishwasher safe. However, note that as soon as a ceramic bowl gets a crack in the surface, bacteria will grow there. If your ceramic bowl develops a crack, throw it out.

Plastic bowls are not a good choice, as some Italian Greyhounds are allergic to the material and will develop a skin reaction on the nose and muzzle. Moreover, scratches on plastic bowls also provide an environment for bacteria to grow.

Collar

Purchase a flat collar for your Italian Greyhound puppy that will fit comfortably. Italian Greyhound puppies grow quickly so most people purchase a nylon collar for a young puppy instead of purchasing an expensive one that will quickly be outgrown. The general rule for the puppy's comfort is a collar that will allow you to put two fingers between the collar and your puppy's throat.

Leash

You can easily buy a leash that matches your puppy's collar. Remember to use a leash that is comfortable in your hand as well as sturdy. Although you will not need it right away, you may want to purchase a 20-foot (240 inches) lead for teaching the "come" cue later. A 6-foot flat leash should be sufficient for now.

Dog Grooming Items

While you do not need every type of dog grooming item available, it is important to have the minimum items for grooming. These include:

a) A set of brushes (Undercoat/Long Hair/Slicker Brush)

b) Nail Clippers

c) Styptic Powder

d) Toothbrush and Toothpaste

e) Dog Shampoo

f) Dog Conditioner

Most pet stores do not have a comprehensive selection of grooming tools, but you can find some of them at pet super stores. You may need to check online to find some grooming tools. This is especially true if you want to find a good selection of dog shampoos and conditioners.

Crate

A crate is a good idea for an Italian Greyhound. Crates are especially helpful during house training. In addition, they will keep your puppy safe when you cannot be there to watch it. Crates are not puppy prisons.

They are your dog's den and most XXX puppies/adults enjoy spending time in them. They also provide a safe place for relaxation and sleep.

In order to determine the size of crate you need for your Italian Greyhound puppy, think about their size as a fully-grown dog. The general rule of thumb is a crate needs to be large enough to allow your fully-grown Italian Greyhound to both lie down and stand up and turn around comfortably inside.

Give your puppy something soft for it to lie on in the crate. A faux sheep-skin mat is popular with many owners and their Italian Greyhounds. If you prefer, you can use some soft, fleece blankets. Fleece is warm, light and soft, making a comfortable and easy-to-wash bed for a puppy or adult Italian Greyhound. Some cheap towels are also sufficient. Always assume that anything you give a puppy has a significant chance of being destroyed.

The effective use of any crate requires training. Your puppy should always be rewarded for going into the crate, and should never be forced into it.

One word of caution: never crate your Italian Greyhound with its collar on. It is quite easy for the pup's collar to catch on the crate bars and choke it.

Choosing a Crate

There are many different kinds of crates. You can choose a hard plastic crate that is used for airline travel. These crates are a good choice if you travel with your Italian Greyhound in your personal vehicle since they provide protection while on the road. Alternatively, you can choose a wire crate. These crates are lightweight and easy to fold up and carry. They are a good choice for people who go to shows, obedience trials, and other events. You can also choose a canvas crate, but these are not generally recommended for Italian Greyhounds that like to use their claws to tear their way out of things.

Dog Bed

Some Italian Greyhound owners choose a dog bed instead of a crate as a place for their pooch to rest. This is fine, but it does not offer the advantages of a crate as a tool in house training. It is recommended that you discourage your Italian Greyhound from jumping up onto your bed or other furniture from the start. This will also help avoid back problems in the future.

Toys

Toys are a necessity for Italian Greyhounds and for the safety of your personal items, too. When your puppy begins chewing on your favorite slippers, reach for a toy to distract your Italian Greyhound from ruining them. If you have ever had a puppy chew your furniture, you will already recognize that it is better to spend a little money on toys than a lot of money repairing your living room.

Make sure you choose toys that are recommended for the Italian Greyhound's breed and size. Start with chew-toys made especially for puppies. Italian Greyhound puppy teeth are sharp and they can quickly destroy toys not made for chewing and choke on the shredded pieces.

Do not shower your Italian Greyhound with lots of toys. Buy two or three and when it gets bored with one toy, bring out another one. Rotating toys like this is the best way to keep them interesting.

Cleaning Supplies

Cleaning supplies are a necessity for homes expecting a new Italian Greyhound puppy. You should purchase carpet and floor cleaners for accidents. These cleaners contain special enzymes that repel dogs and help prevent further soiling. Do not forget to stock up on paper towels. You will need them.

Additional Supplies

In addition to the general supplies you will need for your puppy, there are a few additional supplies you can purchase. Remember, these are optional supplies and you should buy them only if you feel it is necessary.

Puppy Training Pads (Pee Pads)

These are pads for your puppy to use as a toilet indoors or outdoors. The Pee Pad products have a water-proof plastic lining and a special chemical odor to encourage puppies and older Italian Greyhounds to use them. These pads are very useful during the early stages of toilet-training.

Baby Gates

Baby or pet gates are a good way to close off some of your rooms when your puppy comes home. Once your puppy is older and more trustworthy in the home (e.g. it does not eat the buttons off your clothes), you can put the baby gates away if you like.

Some people use gates all the time to keep dogs out of certain parts of the home. For instance, you should not allow your Italian Greyhound to be in the kitchen when you are cooking and eating meals. Pet gates are handy for discouraging this behavior.

Stress Reducing Items

Some owners like to use stress reducing blankets, toys and sprays for their puppies. Alternatively, simply take a small doggie blanket to the breeder's home and have them rub it on your Italian Greyhound puppy's mother and siblings. This will provide your puppy with the same comfort.

Vitamins and dietary supplements

While there can be benefits to giving an adult or senior Italian Greyhound vitamins or supplements, you should never do this without the direction of your vet. Some vitamins are toxic when given in high doses so you want to avoid inadvertently poisoning your Italian Greyhound. Giving vitamins and supplements to puppies is not advised. Giving your puppy additional vitamins and minerals can cause musculoskeletal problems later. This is particularly true with giant breeds.

When you are choosing your puppy supplies, take your time and start with the essentials, as well as food and treats. After that, anything else is just an added way to spoil your puppy.

Puppy-Proofing Your Home

Puppy-proofing your home is a good way to ensure you and your Italian Greyhound get off to a good start. Otherwise, it could cheerfully destroy your house while exploring it.

Put away any hazardous items

1) Household cleaners

2) Vitamin pills

3) Medication

4) Vehicle maintenance liquids such as antifreeze

5) Salts for ice or water softening

6) Pool-cleaning chemicals

7) Tobacco products

Puppy's eye view

Take the time to crawl around your home before your puppy arrives and once or twice a week afterwards. Look at things from your puppy's perspective. Pick up small clips, tags, paper and anything that could be a choking hazard.

Do not let anyone leave their clothes on the floor. Some articles of clothing, such as socks, can pose a choking hazard for your Italian Greyhound.

Put knick-knacks away

Remove any ornaments that you care about until your puppy is older. Wagging tails have a way of knocking everything off a coffee table.

Puppies also like to explore by putting things in their mouths. Putting your objects away will prevent the item from being a choking hazard. It does not have to be permanent, when your puppy is well-trained, you will be able to put things back as they were.

Close off access to standing water

Close toilet seat lids, drain tubs and sinks, and block off any access to a pool if you have one. Standing water can be very tempting for an Italian Greyhound. However, young puppies cannot swim well and falling into the water could lead to a drowning.

Electricity cables and curtain/blind cords

Always tape up your electrical cables out of reach of your puppy, as they like to chew them. Remove any cables that dangle from furniture, such as from a table lamp. Your Italian Greyhound puppy may pull a heavy lamp down on itself while playing with the cable. Ensure all computer and phone cables are tucked away. Pin up any cords hanging from curtains or window-blinds. These can cause strangulation if the puppy becomes tangled in them.

Kitchen waste

Another tempting item for puppies is the garbage can. Always keep it placed out of your puppy's reach, and make sure you empty it every night. This is especially important if your puppy is not sleeping in its crate.

Block off staircases

Due to a lack of coordination, it is quite common for puppies to fall down staircases. In order to prevent this, always block off your stairs at both the top and the bottom with pet or baby gates.

Keep doors closed

Any door or window leading to the outside should be kept closed if the puppy can access it. An open door can be irresistible for a puppy.

Check the Outdoors

In addition to puppy-proofing your home, check your garden or yard carefully. Look for openings in the fence and garden tools that could pose a danger to your Italian Greyhound puppy. If there are any open drains, put a tight-fitting drain cover over them. Cover ponds and pools and remove any items that could be a danger to an inquisitive and energetic Italian Greyhound.

Look at your plants

Finally, look at the plants you have in your home and garden. Many houseplants are poisonous to dogs, so avoid having them in your home. If you have any poisonous plants in your garden, remove them or fence them off so your puppy cannot reach them.

Puppy-proofing is simply keeping your home neat and tidy – and taking a few extra precautions. Ask everyone in your home to pitch in, so your puppy has a clean and safe environment to grow up in.

Toxic Plants

Below is a list of indoor and outdoor plants that you should remove or fence off in your home, or on your property, as they are poisonous in varying degrees.

A

Aconite, Aloe Vera, Amaryllis, Apple Leaf Croton, Arrow grasses, Asparagus Fern, Atropa belladonna, Autumn Crocus, Azalea.

B

Baby's breath, Baneberry, Bird of Paradise, Black Locust, Bloodroot, Box, Branching Ivy, Buckeye, Buddhist Pine, Buttercup.

C

Caladium, Calla Lilly, Carolina Jessamine, Castor Bean, Ceriman, Charming Dieffenbachia, Cherry Tree, Chinaberry Tree, Chinese Evergreen, Chokecherries, Christmas Berry, Christmas Rose, Cineraria, Clematis, Common Privet, Cordatum, Corn Cockle, Corn Plant, Cornstalk Plant, Cowbane, Cow Cockle, Cowslip, Croton, Cuban Laurel, Cutleaf Philodendron, Cycads, Cyclamen.

D

Daffodil, Daphne, Death Camas, Delphinium, Devil's Ivy, Dieffenbachia, Dracaena Palm, Dragon Tree, Dumb Cane, Dutchman's Breeches

E

Elephant's Ears, Emerald Feather, English Ivy, Eucalyptus, European Bittersweet.

F

False Flax, False Hellebore, Fan Weed, Fiddle-leaf Fig, Field Peppergrass, Florida Beauty, Foxglove, Fruit Salad Plant.

G

Geranium, German Ivy, Giant Dumb Cane, Glacier Ivy, Gold Dust Dracaena, Golden Pothos,

H

Hahn's Self-Branching Ivy, Heartland, Holly, Horse Chestnut, Horse Nettle, Hurricane Plant.

I

Indian Rubber Plant, Iris.

J

Jack-in-the-Pulpit, Japanese Show Lily, Jatropha, Jerusalem Cherry, Jimsonweed

K

Kalan Choe

L

Labarum, Lacey Tree Philodendron, Lantana, Laurels, Lily of the Valley, Lupines.

M

Madagascar Dragon Tree, Manchineel Tree, Marble Queen, Marijuana, Matriony Vine, May Apple, Mexican Breadfruit, Milk Vetch, Miniature Croton, Mistletoe, Monk's Hood, Moonseed, Morning Glory, Mother-in-Law's Tongue, Mountain Mahogany, Mustards.

N

Narcissus, Needlepoint Ivy, Nephthytis, Nightshade.

O

Oaks, Oleander, Onions, Oriental Lily.

P

Peace Lily, Peach Tree, Pencil Cactus, Philodendrons, Plumosa Fern, Pokeweed, Poinsettia, Poison Hemlock, Poison Ivy, Poison Oak, Potato Plant, Pothos, Precatory Bean, Primrose,

R

Rattle box, Red Emerald, Red Princess, Red-Margined Dracaena, Rhododendron, Rhubarb, Ribbon Plant, Rosary Pea.

S

Saddle Leaf Philodendron, Sago Palm, Satin Pothos, Schefflera, Skunk Cabbage, Silver Pothos, Smartweeds, Snow-on-the-Mountain, Sorghum, Spotted Dumb Cane, Star of Bethlehem, String of Pearls, Striped Dracaena, Sweetheart Ivy, Swiss Cheese Plant.

T

Taro Vine, Tiger Lily, Tomato Plant, Tree Philodendron, Tropic Snow Dieffenbachia.

V

Velvet Grass.

W

Weeping Fig, Wild Black Cherry, Wild Radish, Wisteria, Wood Aster.

Y

Yellow Jessamine, Yellow Oleander, Yellow Pine Flax, Yew

Chapter Three: Bringing Your Italian Greyhound Puppy Home

The Day of Pickup

The day you pick up your Italian Greyhound puppy is always exciting, especially if you have had a long wait. It can be difficult to stay calm, but it is important to do so for the sake of your puppy. It will be nervous and frightened during this huge change. When you are calm, it is reassuring to your puppy.

To make the transition smooth, send a blanket to the breeder a few days ahead of time and ask them to rub it on the puppy's siblings and mother. If that is not possible, take a blanket with you when you collect your Italian Greyhound puppy. Rub your natural sweat smell on it and at the kennels, rub that blanket on the mother and siblings. This will help your puppy to associate you with the comforting smells of its family.

Leave children at home

It is usually best to leave your children at home when you pick up a new Italian Greyhound puppy. This is true whether you are picking the puppy up at the breeder's home or going to the airport. Moving to a new home is a stressful time for an Italian Greyhound and the excitement of children can greatly increase its anxiety.

Before you leave home, have everything set up so you can simply place your Italian Greyhound in its "safe place" in the crate with the comfort blanket.

Airport pick-up

In some cases, you may be picking up a puppy at the airport, especially if you have found a breeder that lives a long distance from you. If this is the case, you and the breeder should discuss everything over the phone ahead of time in detail.

Puppies traveling by air must have all of the available health certificates and vaccination records, as well as other travel papers. Ensure the breeder sends you the puppy's travel information in good time, so you know where and when your puppy is arriving.

Different airlines handle shipping dogs in different ways, so it is a good idea to call the airline in advance and make sure you have all the correct details. Do note however, in rare instances, airlines have killed animals in cargo. Even when a dog fairs well in cargo, for an 8-12 month old puppy, it is certainly a traumatic experience that it will remember for a long time, so bear this in mind.

Some countries require quarantine procedures when a dog enters the country. Be sure to find out if your country requires any kind of quarantine for when dogs are imported.

Fresh water and toilet break

Dogs can and do get lost at airports, so resist the temptation to open your Italian Greyhound puppy's crate as soon as you see it. Wait until you have the crate safely secured in your vehicle before you open the door.

Give your puppy some fresh water to drink and then put on the collar and lead. As soon as you can, visit a suitable rest area where your puppy can relieve itself, and offer it some more fresh water.

Try to plan ahead, so you can stop at a secluded spot and avoid contact with other dogs. This is to prevent infection from unvaccinated dogs that may be carriers of disease. Let your puppy eliminate and then pick it up immediately and put it back into its travel crate.

Picking up at the breeder

At the breeder's house, spend some time with your puppy, its litter-mates, its mother, and with the breeder. Have any last-minute questions written down so you do not forget them. Maintaining a good relationship with your puppy's breeder is important. They will be a valuable resource for you throughout your puppy's life.

Car Safety

You should not allow your Italian Greyhound puppy to sit on the driver's lap or be loose in the car, where they are bound to distract the driver and make safe driving impossible. If you are picking your puppy up from the breeder's house, be sure to arrive equipped with a travel crate.

On the way home

After you leave the breeder's home, or collect your puppy from an airport, where possible, try to go straight home. Do not stop to visit a friend or go to a pet store. At this age, your puppy is very susceptible to disease, and stop-offs will expose it to danger and cause extra stress. Try to keep your puppy calm and do not worry about showing it off just yet, your puppy will soon be able to go out and visit friends with you.

Car sickness

Keep an eye on your Italian Greyhound puppy in the car. Many puppies experience motion sickness in cars. It is possible that your puppy has already taken some car trips to the vet, and this may help, but it will not rule out the possibility of motion sickness.

If you see your puppy's nose drooping towards the floor, with drooling and wrinkling of the lips, it is preparing to vomit. Be prepared to stop the car and allow for a break in order for it to get over its motion sickness.

Crating your puppy during car rides is safer for the puppy and cleaner if it vomits. You may also want to cover your car upholstery with a large plastic sheet that can be disposed of later on. Or take some paper towels and cleaner with you.

At home for the first time

When you get home, take your puppy outside immediately to relieve itself in the area you have chosen. For more information on potty training, refer to the chapter on Socializing and Training.

Once your puppy has finished eliminating, take it inside the home and go to a quiet room together. Sit with your Italian Greyhound puppy and let it explore its new surroundings. Some Italian Greyhound puppies will want to play and run around, others will want to sleep in their crate. Follow your puppy's cues.

Keep your puppy confined to one area at first. Then slowly open up your home as it becomes more confident and trustworthy in terms of house training. The key to introducing your puppy to its new home successfully is being calm, progressing slowly and creating rules and schedules to make it feel secure and to help your puppy know when and where it is supposed to potty.

Introducing Your Italian Greyhound to Family and Friends

During the first few days you will find your Italian Greyhound sleeps a lot. This is normal for all puppies at a young age. However, this will change as it becomes familiar with its home and as it gets older and gains confidence.

Take it slowly

While your first instinct is probably to rush on and introduce it to everyone you know, take note that your Italian Greyhound can become very frightened by too much attention all at once. A puppy can withdraw and "shut down" when overwhelmed by new surroundings or too many people. Since you want all introductions to be positive, make them as calmly as possible.

After allowing your puppy to rest in a quiet room, begin taking your fellow residents into the room to meet it – one at a time. Other animals in the home can wait a day or two. There is no rush. Making the introductions properly will prevent any lasting problems for your Italian Greyhound.

Children and Your Italian Greyhound puppy

It is a good idea to introduce younger children to your Italian Greyhound puppy one at a time. This will help minimize the amount of stimulation the puppy has. If you have older children, you can introduce them together. Start by having your child come into the room and sit down on the floor. Do not rush the puppy or place the puppy in your child's lap. Instead, give your child treats to feed the puppy and allow the puppy to approach on its own terms. Tell the child to stay calm and quiet so the puppy does not become frightened. When the puppy does greet the child, let the child pet the Italian Greyhound calmly.

Keep meetings short and build up their length over the first few days. Supervise all interactions with the children to maintain a calm and quiet atmosphere. As the puppy gets used to the sounds of children, you can start introducing play times.

It is important that children should have rules regarding your puppy and they should be taught how to treat it. Make sure your children understand the following rules:

1) Be calm around the puppy

2) Do not hold onto it when it wants to go

3) Never hit or punch the puppy

4) Do not pull on its ears or tail

5) Gently pet the puppy

6) Use toys to play with the puppy

7) Do not try to take toys or food away from the puppy or dog

8) Do not run away from the puppy or dog

Most Italian Greyhound puppies and dogs do not respect children in the same way they do the adult (taller) members of the family. Your children will not be able to cue your puppy with the same authority that you have until they are a little older.

It is important that an adult is always present to supervise small children playing with, or nearby, puppies and dogs to keep accidents from happening. Once your children are a little older, your dog will respect them more and play is less likely to get out of hand.

As you train your Italian Greyhound puppy, you should include your children in the puppy's training and socialization. This will be helpful for both your puppy and your children in the long run.

How to Socialize Your Italian Greyhound Puppy to Other Pets

Remember that animals already in the home may well exhibit behavioral problems owing to jealousy or problems with territory.

Moreover, if you already have other dogs, or dogs that visit your home frequently, take every dog's personality into consideration. Everything will depend on whether the other dog tends to be dominant or submissive. To prevent problems, ensure that the first meetings are short and do not force any relationships. The animals in your home will sort out their hierarchy on their own.

Here are some useful guidelines for pet meetings:

Keep your puppy confined

The first rule is that you should always keep your puppy confined when you take it home. Place your Italian Greyhound in a quiet room. This will keep your new puppy safe and your current pet will not feel directly challenged. When you are taking the puppy out of its room, always confine the current dog - unless you are taking the time to introduce them.

Allow door sniffing

Door sniffing and crate sniffing are important to your puppy, so always allow it time to do this. In addition, you should allow your current pet to sniff at the crate or the door where the puppy is.

a) This will help your pet become acquainted with the puppy, with a safe barrier between pet and puppy.

b) Do not let them be pushy during initial meetings and if your puppy starts to look stressed, stop the interaction straight away.

Setting up a meeting with current pet

1) Plan the meetings between your current pet and the Italian Greyhound puppy in advance.

2) Never take a puppy into the room where your current pet is. Allow the older dog to take charge.

3) Wait until your current pet is calm before you make the introductions. This will help promote a positive experience for both your new Italian Greyhound and your current pet.

4) Encourage your current pet to equate your puppy with positives When you are doing the introductions, always provide the older dog with plenty of affection.

5) Give lots of praise and physical strokes/pats for greeting nicely and make sure you give it plenty of treats.

The more you praise your current pet, the more it will think the new Italian Greyhound puppy is something positive.

Cats

While you can control the meetings between a dog and puppy, it can be difficult to control the meeting between an Italian Greyhound puppy and a cat. Puppies often find cats interesting (too interesting sometimes) and will try to chase the cat or play with it. When this happens, the cat will feel threatened and can react aggressively.

1) The best approach is to let the cat watch the Italian Greyhound puppy from its own vantage points.

2) Praise, treat, and pet the cat when you are able to do so, to keep it feeling comfortable with the new excitement in the home.

3) After a few weeks, start taking your cat down from its perches, to be nearer to the young Italian Greyhound, but only when the puppy is calm.

4) Do not introduce the cat in the middle of a boisterous play session.

5) Always make sure you have full control of your Italian Greyhound puppy, to prevent it chasing the cat.

It may take time, but eventually your Italian Greyhound will make friends with the cat, though it will always be on the cat's terms.

Make the older pet the primary pet

What this means is that your current pet should have more rights than the puppy. The current pet should be fed first, you should greet it first when you get home, and you should always allow the current pet to enter or exit first. If you support your older pet's position, it shows the puppy that it must respect the older pet.

Rights of seniority

You will avoid fights over status and rank if you support your older pet's rights. Your puppy may try to challenge your older pet's authority, but it is up to you to promote your older pet if you want peace in your home. As the animals become used to each other, you can start offering more attention and other things equally, but for the first few months, make the current pet feel extra special.

Occasionally, an older dog may be happy to allow an Italian Greyhound puppy to assume leadership and that always works out very well.

Be patient

Finally, be patient with your pets. Remember that this is a huge change of environment and companionship for them. It can take up to 6 months for the puppy to be accepted by the current pets.

Chapter Four: Caring for Your Italian Greyhound

Caring for your Italian Greyhound need not be overly complicated. In this chapter, we will discuss everything you need to know about taking care of your pooch on a day-to-day basis.

Daily Care

Setting up a daily schedule will help you to care for your Italian Greyhound. Remember, when your puppy is young, it will not be able to be left alone for long periods. You can expect about three to four hours between each potty break. As your Italian Greyhound ages, you will be able to leave it for longer periods without having any accidents in the house.

Your Italian Greyhound's schedule should include the following:

Feeding

Dogs should be fed every day and how often really depends on your Italian Greyhound's age. Puppies usually need to be fed about three times per day when they are young. As your puppy grows older, you can begin to feed it twice a day.

You can also give your Italian Greyhound treats but remember that treats contribute to the daily intake of calories. Too many treats can put pounds on your pup. Small treats are good to use as a reward when you are training your Italian Greyhound. You can use anything your dog likes as a treat. You can also use healthy treats such as pieces of plain cooked, boneless chicken, sliced very small, no larger than one of your incisors.

Watering

Make sure your Italian Greyhound always has access to fresh, clean water. Dogs typically drink more water when the weather is hot, but they should always have water available. Water should be changed and the bowl should be cleaned at least once daily.

Socializing and Training

Every Italian Greyhound should be properly socialized. We will discuss this further in a dedicated chapter, but it is worth mentioning here because it should be part of your puppy's daily routine. Start socialization early and continue it throughout your Italian Greyhound's life.

Training your Italian Greyhound is important in terms of obedience, but it is also a good way to bond with your Italian Greyhound and it keeps it from getting bored. If you spend 15 to 20 minutes per day training and socializing your puppy, you will see positive results.

Bathroom Breaks

Another factor with daily care is taking your Italian Greyhound outside for potty breaks. Puppies can hold their bladder for one hour for every month of age. So an eight-week-old puppy should be taken outside every two hours. Bear in mind that some puppies can hold their bladder longer than others, so this is not a hard-and-fast rule. Also, do not expect your puppy to be fully house trained until it is about 6 months of age.

A puppy will be most likely to eliminate after waking, after eating and after playing. Always reward the puppy for eliminating outside. Once the puppy learns that it can trade outdoor potty visits for treats, it will be housebroken in no time at all.

Adult Italian Greyhounds should be taken out 4 to 5 times a day, if not more. Most owners take their Italian Greyhounds out as soon as they wake up in the morning, after each meal, when they come home from work, and before bed. If you have your own yard, you can allow your dog to spend more time outside and exercise itself, eliminating when necessary.

Quality Time

You should include quality time in your schedule every day. An Italian Greyhound thrives when it can spend time with its owner. This does not have to be time-consuming. Try scheduling time to sit down and pet your puppy while you watch TV, for example.

Daily care can take you all of an hour a day and many of the things you need to do for your Italian Greyhound can be done when you are doing other things. Take the time to make your Italian Greyhound happy, and it will become a wonderful companion you love spending time with.

It is also important to spend quality time outside with your Italian Greyhound. Play fetch, take it to a dog park, or simply do some training in the backyard. The key is to spend some time together outdoors bonding with your Italian Greyhound.

Exercise

Exercise is an important part of caring for your Italian Greyhound and will be one of the deciding factors in how happy your puppy is.

You may get the impression that your dog does not need or want much exercise. However, it could quite possibly be awake at night, guarding the house. Italian Greyhounds should not be left outside at night or they have a tendency to bark at every strange sound – making you unpopular with your neighbors.

You can deter your pup's tendency to sleep all day and stay awake at night by taking it for several long walks during the day. Ensure that you give it sufficient exercise and make it tired enough to sleep at night. Keep in mind that puppies will tire more easily. You should take them out more often and for shorter times.

As mentioned earlier, if you have a fenced garden or yard, you can encourage your Italian Greyhound to spend time outside exercising during the day. Do make sure that you have a secure fence so your pooch will not be tempted to escape. To add to this, checking your fencing regularly to ensure it is in good order is also recommended. You must also add safety to any latches on gates. They WILL be figured out eventually.

Another important aspect of exercise is to exercise your Italian Greyhound's mind. Intelligent dogs can become a handful when they do not have something to do. Give them access to toys when you are away. There are all kinds of toys for dogs today from simple balls and rope toys to more complex toys that challenge a dog's IQ. Provide your

Italian Greyhound with a variety and it is sure to find some to keep it busy.

Grooming

Grooming should be part of your puppy's daily routine. It is good for it and it is a great way to acclimate your puppy to being touched and handled. Take the time to touch its paws, tail, head and body. Make grooming a positive experience with treats and praise. If you start off in this way with your puppy, this activity will always be easy and enjoyable for you both.

Vaccinations

Most breeders will advise you to take your new Italian Greyhound puppy to the vet within 2 – 3 days of taking it home. This is good for you, the breeder and your puppy. If you have a legal contract with the breeder, it probably includes this as a "condition of purchase."

It is important to make sure the puppy is in good health when it arrives at your home. Depending on the puppy's age and its vaccination schedule, you may be able to combine its next vaccinations with its first vet check-up.

Required Vaccinations in Britain

Recommended vaccinations vary slightly, depending on where you live. However, the standard puppy vaccinations in Britain include the following:

a) Canine Parvovirus

b) Canine Distemper

c) Canine Parainfluenza Virus

d) Infectious Canine Hepatitis

Note: Kennel Cough and Leptospirosis are also offered as standard puppy vaccinations, but both are unnecessary. They are only needed if you plan to kennel your Italian Greyhound in close quarters with other dogs.

Coronavirus is considered optional. Rabies is usually only given to dogs in the UK if they are planning a trip abroad since rabies has been eradicated in Great Britain.

Required Vaccinations in the United States

Puppies receive the same vaccinations in the United States, though Leptospirosis is considered optional, depending on where you live. In some areas a vaccination for Lyme disease (spread by ticks) can also be given, but it is not considered a basic vaccination. However, the rabies vaccine is required for dogs by every state, usually by the age of four months old.

Some of these vaccines, such as the parvo vaccine, need to be given several times over the course of several weeks to make sure the puppy is fully immunized. Once your puppy's vaccinations are completed, it will need to have booster shots when it is a year old. After that, the vaccines will need to be updated every two to three years so your puppy will not need to be given all of the vaccinations at the same time again.

For more information on vaccination, please refer to Dr. Jean Dodds Vaccination Protocol.

Chapter Five: Grooming Your Italian Greyhound

Although many people view grooming as a chore, it can actually be a very pleasant activity for you and your Italian Greyhound. It provides you with an opportunity to bond with your pup and also creates a period of quiet time for your Italian Greyhound. In addition, it helps you stay on top of health problems with your Italian Greyhound since part of grooming is checking over their health. You can check its body for any lumps or bumps that might be a cause for concern.

From an early age, train your puppy to lie on its back and on its side to allow for grooming. The time to do this is when your pet has had its exercise for the day and is tired, so it is comfortable lying quietly. Training your Italian Greyhound from a young age to co-operate with grooming sessions will pay huge dividends later on.

Brushing

Italian Greyhounds should be brushed several times per week. Brushing has many benefits:

a) Allows you to bond with your dog.

b) Helps distribute natural oils through your Italian Greyhound's coat.

c) Removes dead skin.

d) Removes dead hair.

e) Allows you an opportunity to check the health of your Italian Greyhound's body.

Brush your Italian Greyhound in the direction of hair growth, not against it. Use smaller brushes and combs for the legs and other parts of the body. Brushing should only take 10 to 20 minutes. End every brushing session with a treat so your pup will look forward to being groomed.

Nail Clipping

You will also need to keep your Italian Greyhound's nails trimmed. If this is something you are uncomfortable doing yourself, veterinarians will often cut nails for their clients or you can visit a pet groomer.

Nail clipping, and the frequency of clipping, differs from Italian Greyhound to Italian Greyhound. Some will require that their nails be clipped once a week, others once a month. Where you live, the flooring and ground outside, and other factors will determine how long the nails grow and how often they need to be trimmed.

To properly clip your Italian Greyhound's nails, you can either use a traditional clipper, which has a sharp blade or a Dremel tool. Dremel tools, which are small sanding devices, keep the nail smooth. If the quick (vein found in each nail) is cut, the Dremel tool can cauterize the cut and prevent bleeding. However, some Italian Greyhounds object to the noise that the Dremel makes. If you plan to use a Dremel on your Italian Greyhound's nails, it helps to begin early when it is a puppy.

Nail clippers are easy to use but you run the risk of cutting the nail too short, which can be painful to your Italian Greyhound. If you cut the nails too short once or twice, your Italian Greyhound can become foot shy and clipping its nails becomes a struggle. Some owners have found that clipping nails can lead to sharp edges which can result in a series of potential hazards.

When you are clipping the nails, hold the paw firmly in one hand. Holding the tool at a 90 degree angle with the nail, grind or make a small cut. Never take a lot of nail off at one time. Instead, make small cuts and slowly work your way back. It is much better to trim a small amount and shorten the nails over the course of several days or weeks than to try and make them too short in one session.

You should be able to see the quick as a pink or grey line in the centre of the nail. This is the main indication that you are close to the quick. If you happen to cut the quick, do not worry. You can stop the bleeding by dipping the nail in cornstarch or styptic powder. Although your Italian Greyhound will yelp in pain, it is important to cut another nail on your pooch before you end the session, so it does not end a nail clipping session on a negative. We recommend giving your Italian

Greyhound a treat and lots of praise as you trim every nail. Let your pup know that getting its nails clipped is something positive. Be lavish with your treats and praise.

Ears

It is important to clean your Italian Greyhound's ears regularly. An ear infection results in a strong odor coming from the ears. Ear infections occur in the ear canal. Mud or other dirt on the inner ear flap is normal. If you see any type of unusual discharge, take your Italian Greyhound to the vet.

Never use any tools smaller than your finger, such as cotton-tipped swabs, to clean the ears. These instruments will often push the debris down into the ear, causing more problems. Instead, buy an appropriate ear cleaning solution from your veterinarian or at the pet store. Soak a cotton ball in the solution. Place the swab into the ear and then massage the base of the ear. Remove the swab and wipe the outside of the ear canal and the overall ear until they are clean. You can repeat this process as long as any debris or wax continues to come up from the ear canal.

Check the inside of the ears for any hair and trim or pull it if there are mats in the hair or hair growing down inside the ear canal. Keeping the ear clear of too much hair allows air to flow to the ear and discourages bacteria from growing, preventing ear infections.

Teeth

The final thing you should attend to for your Italian Greyhound is its teeth. Do bear in mind that it will not need its teeth brushed several times a day. Instead, brush them several times a week. Use a canine toothbrush. If you have not introduced your Italian Greyhound to brushing, start with just the toothbrush without toothpaste.

Never use human toothpaste as it could make your pup sick, and they can contain Xylitol (an artificial sweetener) which is toxic to dogs. Use toothpaste that has been made specifically for dogs instead. You can buy toothbrushes and toothpaste made for dogs at a pet store or online. Most Italian Greyhounds like having their teeth brushed once they are introduced to it. Dog toothpaste is made in flavors such as peanut butter, beef, and chicken. Dogs usually think the toothpaste is a treat. When brushing the teeth, all you need to brush is the outside surface of the teeth. The top of each tooth, as well as the inside of the teeth, are kept clean by its tongue.

If you do not like the idea of brushing your Italian Greyhound's teeth, some people use a spray or add a liquid to their dog's drinking water that will help keep the teeth cleaner. The chemical ingredient is Chlorhexidine Gluconate. It is an antiseptic/antibacterial disinfectant oral rinse. It is often found in mouthwashes. If you wish to use it for your Italian Greyhound, be sure to buy a version made for dogs.

Alternatively, many owners have had much success with feeding their Italian Greyhounds sweet-potato dog chews. They are practical, time saving, and in some cases will do a better job than the owner, equipped with a toothbrush and paste.

Bathing

Italian Greyhounds do not need to be bathed frequently. They do not have much dog odor and their coat tends to shed dirt, so try to avoid frequent bathing. Too much bathing can dry out the skin, removing the coat's natural oils, causing damage and more problems.

Bathing once every two to three months is usually more than enough to keep your Italian Greyhound clean. Before bathing, you should brush your Italian Greyhound to remove any knots or hair. When bathing, use a gentle, cleansing coat shampoo for dogs. Avoid human shampoos as the many chemicals and additives to human shampoo often dry out a dog's coat. You can also use a dog coat conditioner after bathing or a de-tangling accessory for dog coats.

Bathe your Italian Greyhound in warm water. Warm water increases shedding while colder water will inhibit shedding. Even though we are tempted to give a very warm bath in winter, this should be avoided because Italian Greyhounds need to keep their coats. Bath water in the winter should be cool but not freezing cold.

Always rinse the coat completely. Leaving shampoo residue can lead to dandruff. Be sure to use a canine hairdryer that does not heat the air to dry the coat thoroughly. Do not use a normal hairdryer for humans as this will damage your Italian Greyhound's skin.

Chapter Six: Italian Greyhound Socializing and House Training

Socialization is an important aspect of your puppy's life and it actually starts from the moment it is born. Your breeder has probably already been socializing your Italian Greyhound puppy before it comes home with you. Puppies raised in a home learn about vacuums, televisions, music. They meet people and get lots of love and petting from the moment they are born.

Most breeders will take puppies outside to let them experience the grass and other surfaces. Puppies usually go to the vet and meet some friendly strangers there. In addition, your Italian Greyhound puppy's mother and litter mates will also teach it puppy manners, so it has some idea of how to behave with other dogs.

Your Key Role in Socializing

Between 3 to 8 weeks of age, your puppy will have been socialized at the breeder's home. However, after you take your Italian Greyhound puppy home, it is up to you to continue to socialize it. This is especially important between 8 to 16 weeks, as puppies are less fearful and more open to new experiences during this phase.

The Italian Greyhound puppy will start becoming more cautious about new things between the approximate age of 7 to 9 weeks (some puppies earlier and some later than this) and this makes socialization more difficult.

The main problem with this restricted 8 to 16 week old age period is the fact that your Italian Greyhound cannot go many places until it has had the second set of vaccinations. Therefore, your role in the socialization process is vital to your puppy's future health and happiness.

Puppies will continue to go through different stages as they grow and develop, including more fear stages.

The Critical Fear Periods in Puppies

a) Seven to nine weeks

b) Four to six months

c) Approximately eight to nine months

d) Approximately twelve months

e) Approximately fourteen to eighteen months

During these stages your puppy can be fearful of people, places and objects that it already knows. It might bark at very ordinary things. It might shake or hide from something that would not normally bother it. This is all normal behavior for your puppy during these stages and you can help by:

1) Sticking to familiar routines during these times

2) Rewarding positive behavior and trying not to encourage fearful behavior

Puppy-Training Classes

Most professional dog-trainers recommend puppy classes after 16 weeks of age and do not start socialization until after those classes begin. However, although puppy classes are recommended, you should be socializing your puppy well before 16 weeks.

How to begin socializing your puppy

During the first few weeks at home, from 8 to 16 weeks, take the time to socialize your puppy to a range of different stimuli in the home, exposing your puppy to the same as what it experienced at the breeder's home. This includes machines such as a vacuum cleaner, television, music, noise from the washing machine and visitors to your home. Make sure that you touch your puppy and handle it often, so it can become accustomed to your touch.

After your Italian Greyhound puppy is 12 weeks old, or has had its second set of vaccinations, take it to places where puppies and small dogs are welcome and continue its socialization with other dogs.

What do I socialize to?

You may be wondering what you should use to socialize your puppy. While everyone has different living circumstances that will change your socialization stimuli, there are a number of stimuli that your puppy should become accustomed to no matter where you live. Below is a checklist to get you started with socializing your Italian Greyhound:

People:

1) Men - bearded and clean-shaven

2) Bald people

3) Women

4) Children - boys and girls

5) Children playing

6) Toddlers - boys and girls

7) Babies - boys and girls

8) People with glasses, sunglasses and/or hats

9) People with crutches, canes, wheelchairs, walkers or slouched or shuffling people

10) People on roller blades, skateboards, bicycles or scooters or people exercising

11) People of various shapes and sizes: tall, thin, heavy, short, etc.

12) Large and small crowds

13) People in costumes

Objects:

1) Balls of various sizes

2) Mirrors

3) Baby strollers

4) Grocery carts

5) Brooms

6) Dusters

7) Vacuum cleaners

8) Flags

9) Tents

10) Flashlights

11) Television

12) Plastic bags

13) Balloons

14) Ceiling fans

15) Garage doors

Nature:

1) Wind

2) Large and small dogs

3) Puppies

4) Farm animals

5) Birds

6) Small rodents

7) Lizards

Noises:

1) Hammering

2) Construction equipment

3) Lawn mowers

4) Sirens

5) Alarms

6) Dremel tools

7) Fireworks

8) Yelling

9) Cheering

10) Radios

11) Storms

Vehicles:

1) Buses

2) Trains

3) Cars (both while walking and riding in them)

4) Planes (optional)

5) Elevators and escalators

Activities:

1) Visiting the vet

2) Getting nails cut

3) Having all body parts touched

4) Being picked up

5) Wearing a collar, harness, leash

Visitors to your home

Introduce frequent visitors of any age to your Italian Greyhound individually, so it is clear who is "friend" and who is "foe." Your Italian Greyhound will have natural protective instincts toward you and your family members, so making these introductions appropriately is important.

Children

Teach visiting children the same rules you teach your own children about respecting your Italian Greyhound and treating it gently. Make introductions calmly and insist that children act calmly around your Italian Greyhound when meeting it. Always supervise children when they are around your Italian Greyhound.

Infrequent visitors

Repair men/women, party guests and other less frequent visitors will also have to be formally introduced to your Italian Greyhound. Ask them to give your pup a pat or two and a food treat supplied by you and stand close to your visitor to show your Italian Greyhound that they are welcome in your home.

Social training with other dogs

Take your puppy to basic obedience classes, where it will meet other dogs and learn social etiquette. The more social opportunities you provide for your Italian Greyhound, the better it will be with other dogs in general.

Italian Greyhounds are naturally territorial in the home, but on neutral ground they are more open to new people and pets. If you have a local dog-walking area, that is the best way to let your Italian Greyhound mix with other dogs. However, avoid areas where there are large dogs and for safety, always stay in the area reserved for small dogs.

House Training Basics

If you are attentive to your puppy's toileting needs and stick to the basics of Italian Greyhound potty training, it should be fully home trained by the age of 5 to 6 months. House training your Italian Greyhound puppy will be easier if you have purchased from a responsible breeder. This will mean your puppy is used to a clean living space. If you stick closely to this house training schedule for Italian Greyhounds, you should not have much difficulty.

Some Italian Greyhounds need extra reinforcement during adolescence or in adulthood, so be prepared to keep them to a tight schedule and watch them carefully when indoors at this time.

Key toileting times

When house training your Italian Greyhound, the key element is being consistent and sticking to a regular timetable while staying friendly and having a good sense of humor. Allow your puppy access to an outdoor location where it can relieve itself soon after:

a) eating,

b) waking from a nap

c) a play session

With a little planning, you will soon be able to arrange your own necessary outdoor trips to fit in with your Italian Greyhound's house training timetable.

At 12 weeks, Italian Greyhound pups can be expected to wait overnight. However, they do not have the same amount of bladder control as an adult, so it is your responsibility to supervise your puppy during the day to prevent "accidents."

Supervision and creating a safe, clean space

One of the best house training tools is a crate, which creates a safe, small space that a puppy from a good breeder should want to keep clean. It is not in any way cruel to use a crate to protect your puppy from getting into a dangerous situation when you are not supervising its behavior directly.

Although you should be cautious about training your Italian Greyhound puppy solely with food treats, a puppy will learn to walk into a crate quite happily if you give it a treat as soon as it enters for the first few times. Give it a toy to keep it occupied while in its crate. Alternatively, give it a hollow steamed bone with some puppy food packed into it. The puppy will enjoy the challenge of getting the food out.

If your puppy is barking, do not rush to let it out of the crate immediately, as this will only teach it that barking is a good way to control you. Instead, wait for the puppy to stop barking - and then add on a few seconds to be sure your Italian Greyhound knows who is boss - before opening the crate and taking it swiftly outside to the toilet area.

Beginning House Training

After the upset of moving to a new home, the puppy will probably want to use the toilet right away.

1) Before you buy the puppy, it is recommended that you choose a suitable spot for toileting it.

2) As soon as you arrive home, take your puppy to this spot. It will sniff around a little. Praise it for this. Let the puppy relieve itself in the chosen spot, keep praising and give a positive reinforcement reward of its favorite food treat.

3) Afterwards, allow your puppy about 20 minutes of "supervised freedom" indoors, before taking it back to the toilet spot. If no use is made of the toilet area, pop your puppy back into the crate for a nap and when it wakes up, take it to the toilet area again.

4) If you see your puppy preparing to urinate or defecate indoors, just scoop your puppy up and take it straight to the outdoor toilet spot.

5) Keep the toilet area clean.

6) Continue to praise your Italian Greyhound for sniffing and using the designated toilet area, until this behavior becomes automatic for your pup.

Note: Never play with your puppy before it uses the toilet, wait until it has done its duty and then have fun together.

How to deal with accidents

If you discover your puppy has had an "accident" in the home when you were not looking, punishing it afterwards will not achieve anything. Your pet has no way of linking the two events and will be confused. Clean up the mess without letting your puppy see you and always take it outside immediately if it returns to the "accident" site and starts to sniff it. Use enzyme-based cleaners that will rid the area of odor.

As Italian Greyhounds begin to understand the toileting timetable, you can allow them progressively longer periods of indoor free time. However, it is your responsibility to watch your pet all the time, for several months, as it gradually gains control of its elimination habits.

Dealing With House Training Problems

House training with a tether

If an adolescent or adult Italian Greyhound starts having accidents in the home, you can attach the lead and fasten it to a belt around your waist. This is generally known as "tether-training" and it lets you supervise your dog every minute, until the official toilet break. It is a good way to stop any unwanted behaviors, such as sneaking off behind the sofa, and helps build the bond between you and your pet.

Diapers or nappies for older pups or aging Italian Greyhounds

Another way to prevent accidents indoors is to place a diaper or nappy on your older puppy or adult dog. Italian Greyhounds do not like the cold dampness of a soiled diaper, and this encourages them to wait for a toilet break, when you remove the diaper and take them outside. If you try this, remember to cut a hole for the tail.

A newer product called Belly Band™ offers the same advantages of a diaper or nappy, but is washable.

When to consult your vet about house training

If you have been carefully following this potty training guide for two or three weeks, but your puppy's toilet habits have not improved, you should take your Italian Greyhound to see a vet.

It is always a good idea to check there is no physical problem interfering with your pet's house training.

Dealing with adolescent territory marking

Unneutered adolescent males retain the instinct to mark their territory. They do this by leaving little spots of urine around the home. Among Italian Greyhounds, this behavior actually helps keep the peace. They will not understand if you have a negative reaction to this behavior, and scolding may result in your pooch hiding to eliminate.

One of the best ways to avoid this is to have your male neutered well before adolescence begins. The best age to have your male neutered is between 4 to 6 months.

However, if you intend to maintain your Italian Greyhound for breeding, surgery is obviously not an option. Handle urine marking with the same diligence you gave to the initial house training: supervision, controlling scent in the places marked, watching for triggers and praising positive behaviors. Always remember this is a natural instinct for the dog, not a willful act against you.

Marking in older males

If you have an older male with marking problems, the Belly Band™ used with tether-training helps to retrain your pet. Use correction at the same time to make a permanent change in this behavior. This should be a short, sharp pull on the lead accompanied by a specific voice cue. For instance, "do not mark."

Rescue dogs marking

Sometimes adult rescue dogs forget their house training or try to mark their new home. Belly Bands™ are also helpful while they are settling in to a strange, new environment.

Females marking

In addition, females occasionally start marking their territory. Tether-training and voice cue will also teach it not to do this. For further details on tether-training, refer to the section on house training your puppy, in this chapter.

Older Italian Greyhounds and incontinence

Spayed females and neutered males sometimes go on to develop incontinence. This problem need not upset your household, as it can easily be controlled by medication from the vet.

Italian Greyhounds recovering from surgery to treat bladder conditions or kidney stones have their own set of problems. It is normal for them to lack full control until the bladder or kidneys heal and this should be treated with patience and understanding.

As always, if you do not see this situation improving after a couple of weeks, consult your vet to see if anything is amiss.

Chapter Seven: Training Your Italian Greyhound

This chapter deals with important areas of training for your Italian Greyhound including basic rules of training and how to teach your Italian Greyhound to follow basic cues. However this advice does not replace the training of a Certified Professional Dog Trainer. If your means allow for it, we strongly suggest you enroll your Italian Greyhound puppy in puppy kindergarten or puppy preschool classes. We encourage you to follow up with a good basic obedience class when your puppy is a little older. This will also offer ample socialization to your puppy.

Also, should you wish to use one, please do research when hiring a trainer. Not all dog trainers are created equal. Ask about continuing education and any certifications they may have, and what they must do to keep them current. Dog training is a totally unregulated field and anyone at all can call themselves a dog trainer and not be accountable to any organization. There have even been cases of pets dying from abuse, resulting from poor "training" in the United States.

It is best to seek out a trainer who is certified by an independent certifying body that is not monetarily motivated by any manufacturers of training equipment or food. Two fine examples are CCPDT (the Certification Council for Professional Dog Trainers) or IAABC (International Association of Animal Behavior Consultants).

Training Basics

It is important to actively work to engage your Italian Greyhound in a way that is both fulfilling and understandable to it or your puppy will quickly lose interest and find something else to do. This is best achieved with the use of a clicker or the word "Yes!" as a marker of good performance.

Always use a marker to inform the dog that it has performed correctly. You must pair the marker word or the click with the treats by repeatedly clicking or saying the marker word as you deposit treats in the dog's mouth. Through this technique, the dog will learn that the click or the marker word means a treat.

Immediate use of a marker is necessary since dogs only have a memory of their own behavior for approximately half a second after the behavior has occurred. The clicker or marker is a more efficient way to communicate this immediate message than trying to deliver a treat within half a second of the correct behavior. One would have to be a veritable ninja with treats to make this work without the marker!

You can apply the clicker or the marker word to teaching any type of behavior. To illustrate, let us use the example of a collar grab. We use a collar grab to let the dog know that touching the collar is not bad. Often, when a cue is given, such as "come," "sit" or "heel," it is because the owner wants to gain control of the dog. If a dog is not trained to become familiar with having its collar touched, it may get into the habit of running away when its owner does this. To apply the marker to the collar grab, every time you reach down and touch the collar, click or say the marker word and give your dog a treat.

One of our Certified Professional Dog Trainers (Certified Canine Behavior Consultant and Certified Behavioral Adjustment Training Instructor), from New Jersey, U.S. has some useful insights about training:

"I think there are a few elements that are more important than any others. First, you need a clicker. It's a very distinctive sound that when paired effectively with the right food reward, serves as the best communication tool available. You also need to understand that reinforcement is a far larger category than just food. You need the patience of a saint and you need to be 100% committed to getting what you want. Maybe not today, maybe not tomorrow, maybe not next week, but eventually. However long that might be. You need the animal to trust you completely, not just to give rewards, but to step in and remove things that are making it uncomfortable or remove the animal if it becomes too agitated. Feeling safe and secure is extremely important."

Taking this excerpt piece by piece, we will discuss the clicker or the "Yes!" marker first.

1) Have a great deal of treats in your treat pouch or in a bowl out of the dog's reach.

2) Click the clicker and/or say the "Yes!" marker at the same time as you deposit a treat in the dog's mouth.

3) Repeat this continuously, as fast as you can for about 5 to 10 minutes a day for the first week and then once a week thereafter to maintain the association.

If you do this consistently, you will have trained a very effective reward marker and your dog will think the clicker or the word "Yes!" is a motivating sound in its own right.

From the above quote, the reference to "patience" is aimed at highlighting that training does not happen in a day or even a week or a month. If your Italian Greyhound just is not grasping "Down," keep trying. If you still do not achieve success, do something the dog does know, reward for that, and come back to "Down" later. By staying "100% committed to getting what you want," it is meant that these dogs learn more from us than we think. If you settle for less than what you want; your Italian Greyhound will learn that it does not actually have to perform correctly at all.

Remember, if you miss that half-second window immediately after the desired behavior has been performed, the dog will be confused as to why it earned the treat. There also must be a relationship of trust between dog and owner. Your Italian Greyhound needs to be secure in the knowledge that you will not place it in an uncomfortable situation and leave it to its own resources. You must make every effort to manage its state of mind if you want the best results.

Accept that this process may take some time and celebrate small degrees of progress. Italian Greyhounds are smart dogs and can learn quickly. Whether they choose to obey you is another matter. This is where your relationship and trust with your Italian Greyhound become important. If your dog can trust you completely to pay it for its work and make it fun, then you will have little trouble motivating it.

Do not imagine that you can bully your Italian Greyhound into compliance. Italian Greyhounds expect to be companions and partners. The best policy is calm insistence on what you want, never giving up on the goal. This may mean that you revisit an element of the training in order to achieve the desired result.

House Rules

The Italian Greyhound does require rules and it is essential that you be consistent with them. Before you bring your puppy home, think of the rules that you want to have in your house. If you are fine with dogs on the furniture, allow it. If not, do not allow it from the very moment your puppy comes home. If you change your mind, it will confuse your Italian Greyhound when you finally tell it to stay off.

When you are training your Italian Greyhound, be sure to follow these rules:

1. Manners

Always insist on manners. Never under any circumstances allow a puppy to practice behaviors that you would find undesirable in an adult dog. This means that jumping up should never be practiced. If the puppy does jump up, even once, turn your back on it and make like a tree.

Removing your attention from a puppy is a more effective discourager than anything else. If the puppy still continues to jump, confine it to another area and try again in a few minutes. This is a good time to ask your puppy for a "sit" and then reward it. Remember, give the puppy something it can get right.

2. Make it work

Regardless of whether you are giving it food, a treat or praise, you want your Italian Greyhound to work for it. Always give your pup a cue, such as "sit" and "wait" at dinnertime, before you give it some form of reward. This will teach it that it needs to work for things and will also help with manners so it is not jumping or grabbing at things.

3. Be the initiator

Playing, cuddling, and any type of attention should be done at your initiation. Pick up toys (although you can leave out a few to combat chewing) and bring them out for play sessions.

Do not give in if your puppy brings the toys to you and is pushy in forcing you to play. In addition, do not pay attention to your Italian Greyhound if it is jumping or biting at you to get attention. Instead, ignore it until it is sitting politely and then give it the attention.

4. Give your Italian Greyhound its own space

While it can be tempting to keep your Italian Greyhound with you at all times, make sure that you give it its own space as well. Crate training is recommended since it keeps puppies from chewing when you are not home. You can also give your pooch its own bed area.

This area will give it a chance to take a break when the house is too busy or it is tired. In addition, the crate will be a safe place for your puppy which will help in establishing roles in your home. It will feel secure in such a place, and also help it to understand its role in the house.

5. Always have access to its food

Finally, always make sure that you have access to your Italian Greyhound's food dish. When it is a puppy, take the time to have your hands in its dish and also make sure that you feed it a few handfuls. If your Italian Greyhound becomes too pushy when you are in the dish, lift it up and only feed it by hand when it relaxes.

You also want to teach your puppy that the food will be given back to it so that it does not feel that the food has been lost to it. Always give treats when interacting with the food dish! Have everyone in the house do the food dish exercise to prevent food guarding or aggression. Italian Greyhounds often tend to have issues about food. They can guard their food, dump their food, try to gulp it all down at one go, and show other extraordinary behaviors. You may have to work on your puppy's food issues from a young age to help it relax about them.

In the end, when you are training your Italian Greyhound, it comes down to being consistent, firm and making it fun. If you do that, along with providing firm, calm insistence on the behavior you want, you will make progress with training your Italian Greyhound.

Essential Cues

This section is about the essential cues that your Italian Greyhound should know and how to teach them. It is also necessary to recognize that dogs do not understand the concept of "No." They do what they do for their own reasons. Trying to tell a dog that it is wrong for doing something simply does not compute. People say "No" for many different factors, but dogs need the English words we teach them to have only one definite meaning. It is impossible for an Italian Greyhound to grasp a concept that is so global and all-encompassing in scope. So rather than correcting your Italian Greyhound for improper performance, we use positive reinforcement and praise for the things they do right.

We recommend using a small treat that is soft and does not require a lot of chewing for training. Hard treats that need to be chewed break the training session regularly. We want your Italian Greyhound to focus on training, not chewing. Chicken nuggets or Frankfurters make great small treats. Slice them into pieces that are no larger than half the size of your small finger nail. These treats are rich in flavor, and are easy to chew.

It is important that the treats are small because you do not want your Italian Greyhound to fill up too quickly. You need it to stay hungry long enough to pay attention for the entire time you are training. On the same note, do not feed it a big meal just before you start to train it or it will be uninterested in your treats. In fact, it will probably feel like taking a nap.

This part is critically important: You must avoid baiting or bribing your Italian Greyhound into anything except when first learning a behavior. As soon as it grasps what is being asked of it, remove all treats from your hands. You can achieve this by using a treat pouch when you are out or keeping treats high up on shelving when you are home. This is necessary because your pup must be willing to work for a reward and this takes time to teach.

If you continue to bribe your Italian Greyhound for performing, its performance will become dependent on the presence of the bribe. This will not occur if your Italian Greyhound understands the concept of rewards and can trust you to reward it once it has done something right. Performance need not be dependent on the presence of food.

When you are training your Italian Greyhound, keep it on the leash the entire time unless you are practicing off-leash lessons. This will prevent your dog from wandering away if it becomes bored. To prevent boredom, keep your training sessions to about 15 minutes and vary them. In addition, never give a cue more than once. If you do this, your Italian Greyhound will decide that it does not have to listen.

"Sit!"

"Sit" is one of the first cues your Italian Greyhound will need to learn. To train "sit," do the following:

1) Have your dog stand in front of you so it is facing you.

2) Place a treat in your right hand and place it near its nose. Do not let it pounce at the treat.

3) Give the cue, never repeat the cue, just say it once, "Sit."

4) Take the treat up and over its head slowly. Its muzzle should follow and its bottom should drop. Use the click or the marker word to tell your dog it has performed well the instant its bottom touches the ground.

5) BE PATIENT, it may take a while to achieve the behavior you want. NEVER force your Italian Greyhound to do anything as this will engage its oppositional reflex and this will shut down any learning that might have occurred.

6) Just be patient and persistent. If it just is not working, come back to it after a relaxing break.

7) Never punish or correct your Italian Greyhound for an incorrect behavior. This will sour it on the learning experience and can lead to very serious behavioral issues later in life.

If you are having too much difficulty teaching your Italian Greyhound the necessary cues, please contact a Certified Professional Dog Trainer for help.

"Stay!"

"Stay" is another cue that is taught when your puppy is young. It is an important cue that can be used in conjunction with a number of different cues. To train "stay", do the following:

Ask for a "sit" and reward when you receive one. Say the cue word, "stay" and place your hand in front of its nose, palm facing your Italian Greyhound. Count one second and click or say the marker word and give a treat. Gradually increase the duration of the "stay" by waiting three or four seconds between giving the cue and marking then treating. Once it has completed the "stay" successfully several times, start adding distance in by taking a small step backward after you give the "stay" cue.

1) If it does not move, take a step back and praise it, touch its collar and give it a treat.

2) Repeat the process, slowly going further away from it and making it wait for longer as the training progresses.

If it breaks the "stay," do not correct or punish, simply reset the "stay" at an easier level and then work the treats back in. Your calm persistence and clear communication will pay off.

"Down"

Teaching "down" refers to teaching your Italian Greyhound to lie down. This should be taught after your pup has learned the "sit" cue since you will often put them into a "down" from a "sit," especially when they are first learning the cue. To train "down," do the following:

1) Ask your Italian Greyhound for a "sit" so it is facing you. Mark and reward that "sit".

2) Place a treat in your right hand and place it near its nose. Do not let it reach for the treat. Slowly move the treat from its nose to its front toes. It should fold right into a down after a few tries. If you are not having any success, just be patient and stick with it. Your persistence will pay off.

3) When it finally does put its front elbows on the floor, mark the behavior with a click or the marker word and deliver a treat. Repeat several times.

4) When your pup has grasped this maneuver, name the behavior with the "Down" cue. To do this, just say the word "down" as you are clicking or marking on the instant the front elbows touch the ground and your Italian Greyhound is lying down.

5) Gradually begin to say the "down" cue sooner, just before the elbows touch the ground. Continue to click or mark and treat as soon as its elbows touch the ground. As your pup is more successful, begin to say the "down" cue sooner and sooner.

In no time, you will have a good grasp of the "down" cue.

6) Remember, this can take weeks of trying for some Italian Greyhounds to learn. Never use force to mould an Italian Greyhound into position.

7) When it is lying down, give your Italian Greyhound praise, touch its collar and give it a treat.

"Come"

This is one of the most important cues that you can teach your Italian Greyhound, and is also one of the hardest. This is the cue where you will need to have some trust in your dog. However, when you are first training your Italian Greyhound, you will need to keep it on the long leash.

When you are teaching "come," it is important to never use this cue for punishment. What this means is that you should never tell your Italian Greyhound to "come" when it has done something wrong, and then punish it when it does. It will learn that "come" is a bad thing and will not "come" at any other time. Instead, make it the most wonderful thing that your pup can do. Heap praise on it and give it lots of treats. To encourage your Italian Greyhound to "come," clap your hands, be exciting and interesting and it will come running.

You can train "come" in two different ways, one is when you place your puppy in a "sit" and "stay," and then call it to "come." This is a focused "come" and while it is useful, it should not be the only way you teach "come." Remember that 90% of the time, your Italian Greyhound will need to come when there is something more interesting to look at. The other way to train "come" is when it is distracted. This can be taught on a leash as well. To do any type of leash training to "come," you should do the following:

1) Place your Italian Greyhound on the leash. Either have it do a "sit"-"stay" or let it forage out ahead of you. A 50-foot lead is recommended for this so you can introduce "come" at different distances.

2) If it is in a "sit"-"stay," walk away from your Italian Greyhound and then give the cue for "come." If it is forging ahead, wait until it is distracted.

3) Give the cue, "come," and then encourage the dog to come to you by clapping your thighs, being excited and so on. Wave a treat out for it. Do not repeat the cue.

4) Simply walk in the opposite direction. This may pull the leash tight, but remember, once the dog decides to join you, shower it with praise and treats.

5) When your Italian Greyhound reaches you, either on its own or by being reeled in, use the treat to guide it into a "sit" without giving the cue.

6) Praise the dog, touch its collar and treat.

7) Continue training "come" over several weeks. After your puppy becomes adept at "come" at a few feet, increase the distance slightly. The goal is to work up until it can be 100 or more feet from you and still "come" when called, whether on the leash or off.

"Heel"

Many owners have problems with dogs that drag them down the street, pulling their arms out of their sockets, and tangling leashes around legs. It can be dangerous to take a walk with some dogs because of this.

Heeling and walking on a loose leash are two different things. Heeling is more formal and it requires the dog to walk politely at your left side, at knee-level, and sit when you stop walking. It is a cue that is often seen in obedience classes and obedience tests.

Walking on a loose leash is a more informal cue in which the dog walks politely on the leash without pulling, and is not required to stay exactly by the owner's leg, or to sit when the owner stops walking, but it must not pull on the leash or be rambunctious. A well-trained Italian Greyhound should be able to heel when asked and always walk on a loose leash at other times.

We will go over training for both of these cues. Heeling first:

To teach your Italian Greyhound to heel you should do the following:

1) Put it on the leash.

2) Set off walking with it on your left side and give the "heel" cue.

3) You should have a large cooking spoon in your left hand. The spoon should contain peanut butter, cream cheese, or some other soft treat that will stay on the spoon. Keep the spoon raised.

4) Every two or three steps lower the spoon and allow your Italian Greyhound to lick the soft treat. Then raise the spoon. Do not break your stride. Continue walking.

5) Stop walking. When you are first teaching this cue, you will need to give your Italian Greyhound the "sit" cue when you stop. Eventually it should sit on its own each time you stop.

6) When you stop and your dog sits, let it lick the spoon again. Praise it.

7) Give the "heel" cue and start walking again. Repeat.

This is a very popular method of teaching how to heel, and it works. Your Italian Greyhound will be glued to your side while you have that spoon – long enough to learn the cue and what it means. You can gradually stop using the spoon and the soft treat. This method is a lot more fun for your dog than the endless repetitions of the traditional way of teaching a dog to heel, or using a corrective collar.

Walking on a Loose Leash

Walking on a loose leash is not a cue as much as it is an expectation. We all expect our Italian Greyhounds to have good manners. This includes when we are out in public with them, walking down the street or visiting someone.

Leash skills begin in puppyhood. This is where your Italian Greyhound puppy will learn what a leash is and how to behave while on it and off it. There are several rules to follow when teaching a puppy basic leash manners.

First, understand that the leash pulls both ways. However, it should never be used as a communication device by jerking or hauling the puppy around with it. If you jerk or haul with the leash, the puppy will learn that the leash means negative actions are on the way.

Second, always treat the leash like a piece of thread; as if it will snap if it is pulled too hard either by the puppy or by you. This will establish an understanding between you and your puppy that goes something like this. "I won't pull the leash too hard if you do not pull the leash too hard." Once this is understood, everything else becomes much easier.

Finally, refrain from using your arm muscles to manipulate the leash. Instead, it is much better to plant your hand in one position (such as your belt line) and use your body to communicate motion to your Italian Greyhound. This is because dogs rarely pay attention to anything above our abdomens. Therefore, it is more effective to use your feet and legs to communicate what you want the puppy to follow, than it is to move your arms.

There are several variations of teaching your Italian Greyhound to walk on a loose leash, and they all use the same principle: keep your dog guessing. Here is the most basic version.

The Three Iron Rules of Loose Leash Walking

There are only three simple rules to follow for loose leash walking.

1) Your Italian Greyhound must never be allowed to get away with pulling. If there is pulling, stop the forward motion immediately. The dog may only go forward if it does so nicely.

2) If pulling continues, walk backwards. It must learn that pulling gets it the opposite of what it wants. Be careful to never jerk or use your arm muscles to pull the leash. Your rearward motion will do a much better job of convincing your Italian Greyhound to join you.

3) Success depends on utter consistency. If you decide that your Italian Greyhound can pull because you are heading in that direction anyway, you have just ruined whatever progress you might have made and you must now start again, back at the very beginning.

Advanced Cues

Once your Italian Greyhound has started learning some of the basic cues, you can start adding in some of the more advanced cues. These cues are often useful in everyday life or if you intend to get involved in dog events and activities.

You can teach it a wide variety of cues, depending on what you are interested in doing with your Italian Greyhound.

"Focus" (This should ideally be your Italian Greyhound's name)

Not everyone teaches "focus" but it is useful because it is just a quick reminder to your Italian Greyhound that they need to focus on their handler. To teach "focus," all you need is a treat.

1) Have your Italian Greyhound sit or stand in front of you.

2) Place a treat in your hand and place it against its nose. Do not let your puppy take the treat.

3) Raise the treat slowly to your face, near your eyes.

4) Give the cue, either by saying your Italian Greyhound's name or "Focus" or "Watch."

5) When it makes eye contact, praise and then give the treat.

6) Remove the treat from your hand and continue rewarding for eye contact. You should practice this in different locations, such as the dog park or in your yard. Be sure to remember that it does not have to "come," it just has to pay attention to you. It is acceptable to toss your treat to your Italian Greyhound if it has paid attention to you at distance.

"Drop It"

"Drop it" can be a life-saving cue since it will teach your Italian Greyhound to drop anything that you do not want it to have. "Drop it" is quite easy to teach but you need to set your pup up for the exercise or wait for it to have something that you need to take. To train "drop it," do the following:

1) Have your Italian Greyhound grab something with its mouth. Playing fetch is a great way to encourage this.

2) Once it has something in its mouth, grab the object with one hand. In the other, have a treat.

3) Give the cue, "Drop It."

4) Place the treat near its nose so your puppy can smell it. Your puppy should drop the item.

5) If it does, praise and treat.

6) If it does not drop the object, stuff the treat in its mouth behind the item, this will get your puppy to drop it.

7) When it drops the item, act like your puppy performed without having food inserted into its mouth; praise and treat.

"Leave It"

Like "Drop It," "Leave It" is another cue that could save your Italian Greyhound's life. Teaching them to leave things alone on the ground will keep them from eating dangerous items on walks. To teach "Leave It," you want to work in stages. Start by leaving things in your hands and then moving up to leaving things on the ground.

1) Place a treat in your hand and close your fist.

2) Hold it in front of your Italian Greyhound and give the cue, "Leave It."

3) Allow it to sniff the treat and try to get at it but ignore it when it is doing this.

4) Once it stops, even for a second, praise your Italian Greyhound and give it a treat with your other hand. Do not give the treat from the hand you told it to leave.

5) Repeat.

6) Increase the difficulty as your Italian Greyhound improves with the cue. Place the treat on your open hand, then on the ground under your cupped hand, and then on the ground without your hand covering. Always treat your Italian Greyhound when it visibly leaves the treat when you give the cue.

These are the basics of training your Italian Greyhound. Remember that training lasts the life of your Italian Greyhound and you should spend time everyday working on different lessons, even when it is fully trained.

Chapter Eight: Feeding Your Italian Greyhound

There are some important decisions to be made about how to feed your Italian Greyhound. Therefore, it is best if owners understand some basic information about dog food and feeding. Providing your Italian Greyhound with the best possible diet goes a long way in boosting its health and keeping it with you for as long as possible.

Cautions

Veterinarians have written about the noticeable decline in dog health over recent decades. Since the 1950's in the U.S. and the 1970's and 80's in Britain, convenience food for dogs has been advertised as healthy food. However, most of these foods contain unhealthy additives and fillers, including high quantities of corn and other bulking agents. These ingredients are not good for dogs, despite the expensive advertisements that present them as "perfectly balanced nutrition" or "luxury food." Grains like cornstarch and oils like corn oil in particular are used to bulk out dog foods, along with lots of extra fat and artificial colors and flavorings. These unhealthy additives often cause illness in dogs.

There is some debate in the veterinary community about whether or not dogs require carbohydrates in their diets – foods such as yellow sweet corn, beetroot pulp or potatoes. Some vets, like Dr. D. S. Kronfeld, say that adult dogs do not need carbohydrates because their liver makes enough glucose from a diet of meat protein and fats. Corn in particular is a problem because it is difficult for dogs to digest. Dogs, which are primarily carnivores, do not have a necessary enzyme – amylase – to digest corn.

Other experts say it is not necessary to eliminate carbohydrates from the diet, arguing that a dog may be as prone to a sensitivity to beef, chicken, lamb, fish, and even eggs and dairy as they might be to ingredients such as corn, wheat or soy.

Note that many commercial dog foods are almost exclusively made with meat that has been ruled "unfit for human consumption." It may no longer be fresh, come from diseased animals or in some other way unusable. This is not the kind of food our furry friends deserve.

Do your own research, talk to your breeder, and make the best decision you can for your Italian Greyhound.

Illnesses related to unhealthy ingredients in food include:

1) Diarrhea

2) Excessive itchiness (hot spots) caused by food allergies

3) Face rubbing

4) Foot licking

5) Hair loss

6) Severe dandruff

7) Upset stomach and passing foul-smelling gas

8) Bladder and kidney stones

9) Premature death

In addition to these concerns, whenever you change food, whether you are feeding a an adult Italian Greyhound or puppy, you need to do so slowly, over several days to avoid stomach upset. You will need to feed your puppy the food it has been used to eating at the breeder's home at first and then slowly make any changes to its diet.

Types of Food

Good dog food always has meat as the main ingredient. Along with muscle meat, like ground beef and chicken breast, it should also contain: heart, liver, kidney, bone or bone meal.

You can generally identify good quality foods by the following factors:

a) Fewer grains (but not necessarily grain-free)

b) Lower carbohydrates

c) Two or three named meats in the first several ingredients

d) Named fats

e) No artificial preservatives, flavorings, sweeteners, or colors/dyes

f) No ingredients with "digests;" better foods contain no meat by-products

g) Human grade ingredients are preferred (though, legally, this is controversial since pet food cannot be sold as human food; but the ingredients should be fit for human consumption before they are made into pet food)

In the United States pet foods should have AAFCO approval (Association of American Feed Control Officials), indicating that they have passed minimum nutritional standards. In Europe, the EU Commission and other entities provide pet food regulations.

In general, most Italian Greyhounds do best on a diet that is high in protein and which has moderate fat. Puppies need to grow slowly. Fast growth can lead to arthritis and other joint problems when the dog is older.

There are five types of food that you can feed your Italian Greyhound;

Dry food

The most common and least expensive food that you can give your Italian Greyhound is dry food. This includes pellets, flaked food, mixes, biscuits, and kibbles. Kibble is very popular. It is easier to store. The disadvantage with this kind of food is it often contains large amounts of fillers, especially corn-based fillers. You can give your Italian Greyhound dry food occasionally, but mash it up with water, if possible, and leave fresh water available.

Wet food is food that usually comes in a can and has the consistency of canned fish. It has a very high moisture level and is usually higher in calories than dry food. It can be more expensive than dry food.

Wet food

Wet food is not practical for most dogs because of its cost. However, you can use it as a topping for your Italian Greyhound's kibble or a special meal. If you regularly feed your Italian Greyhound kibble, and you want to make a special treat of some wet food, remember to adjust the amount of kibble you are feeding. Otherwise your Italian Greyhound could develop a weight problem.

Semi-moist Food

Semi-moist food comes in small pouches and usually has a kibble-like shape in a meaty gravy. Like wet food, it is usually more expensive than dry. It is usually given as a treat since it is quite expensive. It works well when you blend it with dry food as a topping or treat.

Raw Food

Another type of food that you can give your Italian Greyhound is raw food diet. Raw has a lot of benefits including giving your dog high quality nutrients and a lot of variety. You can tailor the food to your individual Italian Greyhound's needs and you can change it slightly to add in fruits and vegetables. In addition to the variety, Italian Greyhounds tend to use more of the raw diet than they do with the dry kibble so it means less waste to be picked up.

The downside to raw is that if you are creating the recipes yourself, you could end up with nutritional deficiencies in your Italian Greyhound's diet.

If you opt for the raw diet, recommended by many Italian Greyhound owners and vets, here's a sample of a typical diet. This would become the diet for life for a fully-grown Italian Greyhound.

a) Finely mashed up ground beef for puppies

b) From 8 weeks of age, add raw minced lamb and beef plus raw eggs three times a week and sardines in oil once a week

c) Around 14 weeks of age add minced chicken

d) Either goat's milk (the nearest you can get to Italian Greyhound mother's milk) or lactose-free milk up to 6 months or a calcium supplement for dogs

What about the risk of salmonella?

There is a risk of salmonella poisoning when you only feed your pet raw food. There is always a risk of raw meat or eggs containing salmonella, E.coli and other toxic bacteria. These can cause fatal illness in humans and dogs.

Home-Cooked Food

A home-cooked, mainly meat diet - with fish - is one that many owners would recommend. Lightly cooked, fresh or frozen meats will retain the essential enzymes and antioxidants needed to keep your pet healthy and disease-free. You can use store-bought frozen meat to cook and keep in the fridge for a day or two. Or buy fresh meat, which you can cook up in a batch of meat stew and then freeze in handy meal-size portions for convenience.

It is important to do the research before feeding any type of food. Consult your breeder and make sure that whatever you choose, it is complete, good quality, and free of chemicals. If you do that, your Italian Greyhound should be healthy.

What Not to Feed your Italian Greyhound

Here are some foods that you should never feed your Italian Greyhound. While some foods are safe for people, there are a range of foods that can have catastrophic effects on your Italian Greyhound if you feed them to it.

Below is a list of specific foods you should avoid giving to your Italian Greyhound, along with the reasons to avoid them:

Alcohol - Can lead to a coma and/or death.

Apple seeds - Contain cyanide and can lead to death.

Artificial sweetener - Can cause low blood sugar, vomiting, collapse and liver failure.

Avocado - May cause vomiting and diarrhea.

Broccoli - When cooked, it can cause gas, which can lead to bloating; feed raw.

Cat food - While not harmful, too much cat food can lead to health problems due to the high protein and fat content.

Cauliflower - When cooked, it can cause gas, which can lead to bloating; feed raw.

Chocolate - Contains caffeine and theobromine and can lead to vomiting and diarrhea; can lead to death if too much is consumed.

Whole cooked chicken - Whole cooked chicken has bones that can splinter, which can lead to an obstruction or laceration in the digestive system.

Citrus oil - May cause vomiting.

Coffee - Contains caffeine and can lead to vomiting and diarrhea; can lead to death if too much is consumed.

Currants - Can cause kidney damage and have even caused death.

Fat trimmings - High fat levels can lead to pancreatitis.

Any fish that has not been deboned - Bones can lacerate the digestive system. In addition, if fed a fish-exclusive diet, it can lead to vitamin B deficiency, which can cause seizures and death. Fish in do food is fine as long as other nutrients are in the ingredients list. Fish skin is also a nutritious treat.

Garlic - In large doses, can cause anemia.

Grapes - Can cause kidney damage and death.

Grapeseed oil - Can cause kidney damage and death.

Gum - Can cause blockages and contains Xylitol, which can damage the liver.

Hops - Can cause increased heart rate, fever, seizures and sometimes death.

Human vitamins - Can damage your Italian Greyhound's liver, kidneys and digestive system.

Macadamia nuts - Toxins in the nuts can cause seizures and death.

Milk - along with other dairy products, can cause diarrhea.

Mushrooms - Can cause shock, shut down multiple body systems and can lead to death.

Onions - Can cause anemia.

Permissions - The seeds lead to intestinal obstructions.

Peaches - The flesh of the peach is fine, but be sure to remove the pit or it can cause an obstruction.

Pork - Contains bones that will splinter, which can lead to an obstruction or laceration in the digestive system.

Plump pits - The flesh of the plum is fine, but be sure to remove the pit or it can cause an obstruction.

Raisin - Can cause kidney damage and death.

Raw eggs - Can cause skin and coat problems since it decreases the absorption of biotin.

Rhubarb leaves - Poisonous, can affect the urinary tract system, digestive system and nervous system.

Salt - Can lead to vomiting, diarrhea, dehydration and seizures. Large quantities can lead to death.

Sugar - Leads to obesity and has been linked to canine diabetes.

Tea - Contains caffeine and can lead to vomiting and diarrhea. Can lead to death if too much is consumed.

Tomato greens/plant - Can cause heart problems in dogs.

Turkey - Cooked turkey has bones that will splinter, which can lead to an obstruction or laceration in the digestive system.

Yeast - Can cause pain, gas and can even cause a rupture in the digestive system, which can result in death.

Vitamins and Supplements

If you make your Italian Greyhound's food at home, you will know you are providing a fully balanced diet containing essential vitamins and minerals for it.

Italian Greyhounds also need Omega 3 and Omega 6 oils, from eating fish like tinned sardines in oil. The Omega oils advertised in processed dog food lose their benefit after being over-processed. They also often end up turning rancid after being stored for extended periods.

Never give your Italian Greyhound any extra vitamins or food supplements without consulting your vet first. What is good for humans can be poisonous for dogs. In particular, do not give your Italian

Greyhound any vitamin C supplements, as they can be damaging to the liver and kidneys. These are often listed on pill bottles or packs as:

a) Ascorbic acid

b) Sodium ascorbate

c) Calcium ascorbate

d) Ascorbal palmitate

Feeding Time

You should feed an Italian Greyhound puppy three times per day: once in the morning, once around lunch time and once in the evening. As your puppy grows, you can begin to leave out the lunch feeding and move to two meals a day. Never feed only one meal a day, as this can cause stomach problems for your Italian Greyhound. If you stick to a fixed schedule of feeding, your pup will also have a regular time for needing the toilet. This makes life a lot easier for owners and more comfortable for your pet.

We advise against leaving food out all day. If there are other pets in the house, they will probably try eating your Italian Greyhound's food. This practice may provoke food-protection aggression and even fighting between your pets. If you have ever had small children you will know exactly what that is like.

Put the food down and walk away, as dogs like to be left alone when they are eating. Leave each meal out for about 20 minutes and then remove it. If your Italian Greyhound has not eaten all of a meal, put it in the fridge inside a clean plastic bag and then make it part of the next scheduled feed. Your Italian Greyhound will soon realize that it should eat up within the 20 minute meal time. Controlling feedings in this way is the best way to keep your pooch fit. If it misses more than one meal because of lack of appetite, contact your vet.

How Much to Feed

Feeding differs depending on the age of your Italian Greyhound, how active it is and the type of food you are feeding. High quality dog foods require less food while low quality foods require more, so your Italian Greyhound can reach the necessary caloric intake. With feeding, it is important to look at the weight of your pup, as well as its energy level and age.

To do this, we have to look at the resting energy requirements. In other words, how many calories your Italian Greyhound is burning when it is resting. From there, we can begin to adjust the amount of food, or calories that we need to feed the pup.

Determining your Italian Greyhound's resting energy requirements (RER) formula is simple:

RER in kcal/day = 30 (body weight in kilograms) + 70

Take your Italian Greyhound's weight in kilograms and multiply it by 30. Then add 70. This can also work if you are using pounds but just be sure to convert the weight into kilograms first. For this example, let's say that you have a 13 pound Italian Greyhound, you would divide 13 by 2.2 for a total of 5.91 or 6 kilograms, if we round up. Then, multiply 6 by 30 for 180 and then add 70 for a total of 250 calories per day. Most dog food bags have the calorie amount for every half cup or cup so you simply divide the calories needed by the calories provided and spread them over the number of meals you are feeding.

For instance, Purina Dog Chow Complete Nutrition has 430 calories for every cup of dog food. So dividing 430 into 250 means that the dog would need slightly more than 1/2 cup of food to meet its caloric intake needs. This is the resting energy requirement for a dog, but this can be mitigated by a number of factors, including pregnancy, activity level or whether the dog is neutered or intact.

You can check the information below to find the multiplier for resting energy requirements, based on your Italian Greyhound's energy level, stage of life and activity:

Weaning to 4 months (x3.0)

4 months to adult (x2.0)

Lactating female (x4.8)

Pregnant female day 1 to 42 (x1.8)

Pregnant female day 42 to whelping (x3.0)

Adult dog, neutered/spayed with normal activity (x1.6)

Adult dog, intact with normal activity (x1.8)

Adult dog with light activity (x2.0)

Adult dog with moderate activity (x3.0)

Adult dog with heavy activity (x4.8)

Adult dog needing weight loss (x1.0)

As you can see, the daily calories can change depending on the individual Italian Greyhound. So if the same Italian Greyhound from above, that needs 250 calories per day, was a lactating female that was nursing puppies, her calories for the day should be 1200 or 2 ¾ cups of Purina Dog Chow.

Fortunately, most dog food companies have already done this math for you. The guidelines that they include on their labels are based on these figures so you can use their suggestions for how much to feed your Italian Greyhound as a starting point. You will need to watch your adult or puppy Italian Greyhound when you start feeding it a dog food, to see if it is gaining or losing weight and its overall condition. You can make adjustments to its portions accordingly.

For RAW feeding, the amounts are slightly different. In addition, it is difficult to determine the calories as it will vary depending on the food you are using. A pound of beef with a 30% blend of organ, meat and bone has about 2600 calories in it, so the Italian Greyhound that weighs 13 pounds only needs about 0.1 pounds of food per day. The reason for this is because the multiplier for the resting energy requirements is higher when feeding raw. For your convenience, find these multipliers below:

Weaning to 4 months (x6.0)

4 months to adult (x4.0)

Lactating female (x8.0)

Pregnant female day 1 to 42 (x4.0)

Pregnant female day 42 to whelping (x6.0)

Adult dog, neutered/spayed with normal activity (x2.0)

Adult dog, intact with normal activity (x2.5)

Adult dog with light activity (x3.0)

Adult dog with moderate activity (x3.5)

Adult dog with heavy activity (x4.0)

Adult dog needing weight loss (x1.5)

Having said all that and crunching numbers, how much to feed in the end will be dictated by the health and weight of your Italian Greyhound. A too-thin Italian Greyhound will require an increase in the caloric intake while an Italian Greyhound you can't feel the ribs on needs to take a reduction. If you are worried that your Italian Greyhound will still be hungry, you can supplement his kibble with low-cal additives, such as green beans, cooked yams, sweet potatoes or other dog-safe foods.

Providing Snacks and Treats

Walk through a pet store and you will see that there are hundreds of different treats for your Italian Greyhound. It can be difficult to know how to select the ones you need for it.

The first thing to bear in mind is that treats are just that - treats. You should never just feed the treats without thinking about the added calories. Yes, even Italian Greyhounds need to watch their waistlines and feeding treats freely can lead to obesity in your pup. It's estimated that over 50% of all dogs are overweight or obese. A general rule of thumb to follow with treats is to only allow them to take up 10% of your Italian Greyhound's daily calories. In addition, always include the calories as part of your pup's daily caloric intake.

Having raised this caution, treats can be an important tool for training your pet's behavior as well as building the bond between you. Low calorie, homemade healthy treats such as a sliver of dried tuna or salmon are best, because they are tasty and will not cause weight gain. It is quite easy to dry bits of fish in the oven when you are cooking family meals.

Here are some tips for selecting treats for your Italian Greyhound:

1. Avoid foods with additives

Avoid feeding your leftover foods that may have additives in them. Also, never feed your Italian Greyhound from the table as this will reinforce begging.

2. Choose Natural Ingredients

When you are purchasing treats from the store, read the ingredients label. Only choose foods that have natural ingredients and avoid foods with processed ingredients.

3. Avoid products made in China

Although most of these products are safe for your Italian Greyhound, it is important to remember that products made in China are not required to follow the same safety restrictions as in some other countries. Many products are made with chemicals that have been linked to liver disease, cancer and that have even resulted in death.

In addition, Chinese companies have issued recalls on treats and food only after killing a few hundred dogs over a period of years. This practice has been allowed to continue, since people are still buying Chinese products. These are risks you do not want to take with your Italian Greyhound.

4. Try to use fresh foods

While we often think of dog treats as bones or manufactured foods, a carrot or a piece of apple can serve as a treat for your Italian Greyhound. In fact, many fruits and vegetables are safe for your Italian Greyhound and make excellent treats.

5. Be Mindful of health benefits

Finally, when you are choosing your treats, think of health options. Many treats have supplements in them that will help prevent arthritis, boost your Italian Greyhound's immune system and a range of other benefits so check the ingredient list for healthy vitamins and to make sure there are no chemicals in the food.

Healthy Snack Options:

Apples (remove seeds), applesauce, apricots (remove pits), baby food (all-natural; make sure it is free of salt), bananas, beef (raw and cooked), beets, blackberries, blueberries, bran cereal, bread (avid nut breads and raisin bread), broccoli (safe when fed raw), Brussels sprouts, cantaloupe, carrots, cauliflower (safe when fed raw), celery, Cheerios cereal, cheese (cheddar is safe), chicken (remove bones if cooked), cottage cheese, cranberries, cream cheese, cucumbers, dog cookies (homemade and store bought), eggs (when cooked), flax seed, green beans, honey, kale, lemons, marrow bones (raw only), mint, nectarines (remove pits), oatmeal, organ meats (heart, liver, kidney, etc.), pasta (cooked), peaches (remove pits), peanut butter, pears, peas, pineapple, plums (remove pits), pumpkin, rice (cooked only), rice cakes, salmon, spinach, squash, strawberries, sweet potatoes, tomatoes, training treats, tuna, turkey (cooked without bones), watermelon, yogurt, zucchini.

Watering

Give your house-trained adult or puppy Italian Greyhound access to water at all times.

To check if your Italian Greyhound has enough water each day, the rule is 1 ounce (oz.) of water for every pound (lb.) of weight or 66 ml for every kilogram of dog.

Generally speaking, young puppies that are not fully house-trained should only be offered water at set times. This will help reduce the number of times they need to go to the bathroom.

Another good rule with young Italian Greyhounds is to pick up the water dish about 2 hours before you go to bed. This will help your puppy make it comfortably through the night without a full bladder.

Chapter Nine: Italian Greyhound Health

Dogs are second only to humans in the number of identified genetic diseases that afflict them. While it is a misconception that purebred dogs are more prone to diseases than mixed breeds, it is true that some kinds of diseases do seem to afflict purebreds more than their mixed breed counterparts.

Breeders continue to seek ways to breed to increase health. It is important to make sure you purchase from a reputable breeder. Reputable breeders will have an Italian Greyhound's parents' health tested before breeding. The following tests are relevant for the Italian Greyhound:

a) Eyes Certified by a board-certified ACVO (American College of Veterinary Ophthalmologists) Ophthalmologist

b) OFA (Orthopedic Foundation for Animals) or PennHip certification for Hip Dysplasia

c) OFA evaluation for elbow dysplasia is optional in the breed.

By purchasing from a breeder that tests their lines for health, you are less likely to run into the hereditary illnesses that can affect the breed. However, even with the best screening, some diseases can still occur. This chapter is about identifying symptoms that can appear as health problems for your Italian Greyhound.

Signs of Illness

Although signs of illness differ depending on the disease or illness affecting an Italian Greyhound, there are some general signs that can warn you when your Italian Greyhound is unwell. When it has any of these symptoms, it is important to seek veterinary care.

One thing that must be stressed with any breed, including the Italian Greyhound, is that often illnesses are sudden and it is very easy for a dog to go from healthy to gravely ill. Make sure you monitor your Italian Greyhound frequently and perform a daily health check.

Your Italian Greyhound may be sick if the following symptoms exhibit:

Bad Breath

Bad breath is often a sign of oral problems but it can also be a sign of other diseases. If your Italian Greyhound has bad breath, and there is no evident root cause for it, schedule an appointment with your vet.

Drooling

Italian Greyhounds, like any other dog, can drool occasionally. Excess drooling is a signal that there could be a health problem. If your Italian Greyhound is drooling a lot, make an appointment to see your vet right away.

Loss of Appetite

Loss of appetite is often one of the first indicators that something is wrong with your Italian Greyhound. With loss of appetite, it is very important to look at your pup's overall eating habits. If your Italian Greyhound is usually a picky eater, missing the occasional meal should not give rise to concern. However, if your pup normally eats heartily and suddenly loses interest in eating, this can be an indication of a problem.

In addition, if you have a female that has not been spayed, she may stop eating around her heat cycles. Pregnancy can also cause a diminished appetite. If your Italian Greyhound hasn't eaten for more than 24 hours, especially if other symptoms are apparent, it is time to consult a vet.

Excessive Thirst

During the cooler seasons, if your pup seems to be drinking large amounts of water, then it could be an indication of disease or dehydration. In general, an Italian Greyhound should drink between 1/2 an ounce to a full ounce of water per pound of body weight.

Changes in Urination

Changes in the color of urine as well as the frequency of urination can indicate a health problem. It is important to note that an increase in urination can be linked to some illnesses while difficulty urinating can indicate other problems.

If you spot blood in the urine, contact your vet immediately.

Skin Problems

If your Italian Greyhound's skin is a bright red or you see flaking skin, this could indicate a problem with its health. In addition, excessive itching could mean it has fleas, some type of mite or an allergy. Eliminate all possible reasons for the skin problems. Note that allergies in Italian Greyhounds can often be alleviated by avoiding corn and wheat in their food diet. High quality, all natural foods are recommended.

Lethargy

Your Italian Greyhound may sleep during the day but it should not be lethargic. As with changes in its appetite, be sure to identify possible reasons why your pup is tired. Note that one possible reason for lethargy in your Italian Greyhound could be over-exercise. Remember that when it is still a puppy, it should be exercised as much as it wishes and allowed to stop when it wants to stop. Over-exercising a puppy can cause damage to its growing body, since growth plates have not yet closed. Lethargy in older Italian Greyhounds can result from a number of conditions. If no reason for your adult Italian Greyhound's lethargy is apparent, contact your vet.

Gum Problems

Although we see gum problems as being linked to teeth or gum disease, they can actually be linked to other serious diseases that can affect your Italian Greyhound. Look for the following symptoms:

a) Swollen Gums: Swollen gums, when accompanied by bad breath, can indicate gum disease or other oral problems.

b) Bright Red Gums: When an Italian Greyhound's gums are bright red, it could be an indication that it is fighting an infection. Exposure to toxins is another reason for bright red gums. It could also be an indication of heatstroke.

c) Blue Gums: Blue gums indicate your Italian Greyhound is lacking oxygen for some reason. Seek immediate veterinary care in this case.

d) Purple Gums: Purple gums are often seen when an Italian Greyhound is experiencing a problem with its blood circulation or when it has gone into shock. Shock can result from a traumatic injury or acute illness and is usually accompanied by other symptoms such as cold extremities, poor mental state, or an increased rate of breathing and/or loss of consciousness. Seek a vet's attention immediately.

e) Grey Gums: Just as with purple gums, when grey gums are seen in an Italian Greyhound, it can indicate either poor blood circulation or shock.

f) Pale Pink Gums: Pale pink gums can be an indication of anemia in your Italian Greyhound.

g) White Gums: Finally, white gums can be an indication of a loss of blood, either externally or internally. Contact your vet immediately.

As you can see, gums are one of the primary indicators of illness in Italian Greyhounds. If the gums are a challenge to assess for whatever reason, you can also check health by looking at the pink portion your Italian Greyhound's lower eyelid.

Changes in Weight

Detecting fluctuations in your Italian Greyhound's weight may not always be easy, since it means charting its weight, but unexpected weight loss or gain in your Italian Greyhound could reveal an underlying condition.

Stiffness of Limbs

Italian Greyhounds are not usually stiff in their limbs. While old age can create some stiffness, there are several diseases that can affect mobility. If you notice your Italian Greyhound experiencing difficulty in getting up, climbing stairs or walking, there may be an underlying problem.

Respiratory Problems

Take note of excessive sneezing, coughing, labored breathing and panting. It could be nothing, but often respiratory problems are an early indication that your Italian Greyhound has a health problem.

Runny Eyes or Nose

If you see any discharge or fluid coming out of your Italian Greyhound's eyes or nose, keep close watch on its symptoms. This can be linked to several conditions including respiratory illnesses.

Vomiting and Gagging

Dogs will gag and vomit without being ill. However, if you see repeated vomiting or your Italian Greyhound has a bowed look and is continually gagging, seek medical help. Vomiting and gagging can be a sign of allergies or could indicate a life-threatening disease. Again, often allergies can be helped by eliminating corn and wheat from your pup's diet.

Fluctuations in Temperature

Finally, if you suspect that your Italian Greyhound's health is compromised, it is important to check its temperature. Temperatures that are too high can indicate a fever, which could be a symptom of a serious disease. Low temperature could indicate other problems such as shock.

Check the temperature with a rectal thermometer or an ear thermometer. Make sure that the Italian Greyhound's temperature falls within the normal range:

a) Rectal Temperature: Rectal temperatures in dogs should be between 100.5 to 102.5°F (38 to 39.2°C)

b) Ear Temperature: Ear temperatures in dogs should be between 100 to 103°F (37.7 to 39.4°C).

If temperatures are lower or higher than normal, seek veterinary help. One exception to the normal temperature range is in pregnant females. Read the chapter on breeding your Italian Greyhound for more information on this.

It is important to note that some symptoms, occurring on their own, may not indicate a health problem. However, if your Italian Greyhound has three or more of the symptoms, you should seek immediate medical care.

Common Health Problems

I. Genetic Health Problems

a) Hip or Elbow Dysplasia

The dog's hip joint is made up of a ball and socket. Genetics and the environment help determine how the joint fits together. If the joint does not fit right or if it begins to deteriorate, the dog can develop hip dysplasia. Hip dysplasia is one of the most common health problems seen in dogs today.

OCD (Osteochondritis dissecans) is an orthopedic condition, brought about by the improper growth of the cartilage in the joints. It is a form of elbow dysplasia. This condition causes painful stiffening of the joints to the point that your Italian Greyhound may be unable to bend its elbow.

It can result in off and on lameness, pain or deterioration of the elbow joints. You can detect this condition as early as 4 to 9 months of age. Over-feeding your puppy with growth formula, calcium, or a high protein diet can contribute to the development of this condition, as can allowing your Italian Greyhound to walk or stand for long periods of time on a concrete surface, or overworking it, especially as a puppy.

Symptoms

Hip dysplasia:

1) Early disease: signs are related to joint looseness or laxity

2) Later disease: signs are related to joint degeneration and osteoarthritis

3) Decreased activity

4) Difficulty rising

5) Reluctance to run, jump, or climb stairs

6) Intermittent or persistent hind-limb lameness, often worse after exercise

7) "Bunny-hopping," or swaying gait

8) Narrow stance in the hind limbs (back legs unnaturally close together)

9) Pain in hip joints

10) Joint looseness or laxity – characteristic of early disease; may not be seen in long-term hip dysplasia due to arthritic changes in the hip joint

11) Grating detected with joint movement

12) Decreased range of motion in the hip joints

13) Loss of muscle mass in thigh muscles

14) Enlargement of shoulder muscles due to more weight being exerted on front legs as dog tries to avoid weight on its hips, leading to extra work for the shoulder muscles and subsequent enlargement of these muscles

Elbow dysplasia:

1) Not all affected Italian Greyhounds will show signs when young

2) Sudden (acute) episode of elbow lameness due to advanced degenerative joint disease in a mature patient are common

3) Intermittent or persistent forelimb lameness that is aggravated by exercise; progresses from stiffness, and noticed only after the dog has been resting

4) Pain when extending or flexing the elbow

5) Tendency for dogs to hold the affected limb away from the body

6) Fluid build-up in the joint

7) Grating of bone and joint with movement may be detected with advanced degenerative joint disease

8) Diminished range of motion

Treatment

Treatment depends on the individual Italian Greyhound and the severity of the condition. In mild cases, you may never know that your pup has any dysplasia. If your Italian Greyhound begins to show stiffness or other signs of arthritis as it ages, you can talk to your vet about mild painkillers, provide a heated, comfortable dog bed, and help your pup avoid stairs and other activities that might overtax it.

However, regular light exercise is good to keep the muscles in shape. Swimming offers very good exercise for older Italian Greyhounds (and for those with hip dysplasia). In rare cases an Italian Greyhound might require surgery, but this is not common.

b) Entropion

Entropion is a genetic condition in which a portion of the eyelid is inverted or folded inward. This can cause an eyelash or hair to irritate and scratch the surface of the eye, leading to corneal ulceration or perforation. Entropion is fairly common and is almost always diagnosed around the time a puppy reaches its first birthday.

Symptoms

Excess tears and/or inner eye inflammation are common signs of entropion. In some cases, eye tics, discharge of mucus/pus, eye inflammation, or even rupture of the cornea can also be typical signs of entropion.

Treatment

Underlying irritants should be removed before any attempt is made to correct the problem surgically. In some cases antibiotics or artificial tears can help with the problem but surgery is often required.

c) Ectropion

Ectropion is a condition in which the margin of the lower eyelid rolls forward, exposing the haw, or pink part of the eye. It can occur in dogs less than one year old. It can come and go in some Italian Greyhounds, occurring when they are tired.

Symptoms

1) Protrusion of the lower eyelid, and exposure of the inner lid

2) Facial staining caused by poor tear drainage

3) History of discharge from conjunctival exposure

4) Recurrent foreign object irritation

5) History of bacterial conjunctivitis

Treatment

A topical lubricant or antibiotic ointment, along with good eye and facial hygiene usually helps most Italian Greyhounds. Surgical treatment may be necessary in some cases.

d) Vaginal Hyperplasia

Vaginal hyperplasia is most common in young females. It is most likely caused by estrogen stimulation during the heat cycle. Vaginal tissue swells and protrudes through the vulva.

Symptoms

1) Protrusion of a round mass of tissue from the vulva

2) Licking of the vulva area

3) Will not allow breeding

4) Painful urination

Treatment

If your Italian Greyhound is able to urinate, treatment may not require hospitalization, but if the mass has caused blockage, medical intervention and/or surgery may be necessary. If surgery is not necessary, your veterinarian will likely advise daily cleaning of the affected area with a saline solution and lubrication, padding of the environment and/or diapers to reduce friction to the affected area and possibly a urinary catheter. Your Italian Greyhound will probably have to wear a collar to keep her from licking irritated tissues.

e) Epilepsy

Juvenile Italian Greyhounds have elevated risk factors for epilepsy. When epilepsy occurs in Italian Greyhounds, it is typically brought about by stress or dietary and metabolic changes.

Symptoms

Seizures usually have a short aura before they begin. At this time your pup may seem frightened and confused. Some dogs hide or seek comfort. When the seizure starts, the dog will fall on its side, become stiff, chomp its jaws, salivate, urinate, defecate, vocalize, and may paddle with its limbs. These actions usually continue for between 30 and 90 seconds.

Seizures usually occur during rest or sleep, so they often occur at night or early in the morning. Most Italian Greyhounds have already recovered by the time the owner takes them to the vet. During a seizure, you should stay back. Your pup is not aware of you and you could be accidentally bitten.

After the seizure, your Italian Greyhound may be confused. It may wander or pace. It may be very thirsty. Some dogs recover right away but it can take up to 24 hours for a complete return to normality.

Treatment

In Italian Greyhounds that start having seizures before they are two years old, there is a good chance of controlling their seizures with medication. Dogs can take anti-epileptic and anti-convulsant medications. One of the side effects is a tendency to become overweight. Your Italian Greyhound may need a diet plan to help it with its weight.

II. Other Health Problems

a) Cancer

Cancer is the number one killer of older dogs, and certainly isn't something unique to Italian Greyhounds, but it is worthy of note because there are steps that can be taken to prevent common cancers in your pup. The single coat of fur on the Italian Greyhound offers little protection from damaging UV rays, increasing the chance of skin cancer. Once skin cancer develops in a dog, internal cancerous tumors often develop as well. Ensure that your Italian Greyhound stays out of direct sunlight as much as possible to avoid increased chance of skin cancer.

Other common cancers can be prevented in your Italian Greyhound by spaying or neutering it at five to six months of age (unless you plan to breed your Italian Greyhound). Spaying or neutering can reduce the chances of cancer, since 85% of cancers originate in the reproductive system.

Good oral care can also reduce the risk of oral cancers. If detected early, experts say half of all cancers in dogs are curable, so keep an eye out for the symptoms listed below.

Symptoms

1) Unusual odors detected from the mouth, nose or rectal area

2) Development of lumps or bumps on or underneath the skin of your Italian Greyhound

3) Unexplained weight loss

4) Loss of appetite

5) Lethargy

6) Coughing, wheezing or shortness of breath after little exercise

7) Changes in behavior: spending less time with you, sudden aggression, limping or struggling during normal activity

8) Open sores that do not heal or abnormal bleeding

9) Frequent vomiting and diarrhea, bloating or distention of the abdomen

10) Pale gums

Treatment

Similar options are available for treatment of canine cancers as for people: radiation and chemotherapy. There has been recent experimentation with immunotherapy tumor vaccines, but this treatment is not yet widely available.

b) Bloat

Bloat, also called GDV (Gastric Dilatation and Volvulus), is the second most common cause of death in dogs. While deep-chested dogs, such as German Shepherds, Great Danes and Dobermans are most at risk, any owner should watch for symptoms. Italian Greyhounds more than seven years old are more susceptible than younger ones.

Bloat is torsion of the stomach, and must be treated by a vet. Bloat occurs rapidly, mortality is high when dogs are not treated quickly, and symptoms are varied and can be difficult to detect. Prompt treatment is crucial, as dogs can die of bloat in a matter of hours after the first symptoms manifest.

Symptoms

1) Uncharacteristic behaviors, such as asking to go out in the middle of the night or licking the air

2) Frequent, usually unsuccessful, attempts to vomit, or unsuccessful attempts to defecate

3) Anxiety and restlessness, refusing to lie or sit down

4) "Hunched" appearance

5) Bloated abdomen that may feel tight (this symptom can be absent)

Treatment

Prevention is important with bloat. Bloat is often brought about by eating habits. Don't allow your Italian Greyhound to eat too rapidly, to exercise for an hour before or after eating, and make sure it has access to fresh drinking water, but only one hour before or after eating.

When switching dog foods, do so gradually. Feed twice a day, rather than once a day. Keeping one of the following products on hand can help relieve gas, extending the time you have to safely find a vet for treatment: Mylanta Gas, Phazyme, Gas-X. Keep the phone number of a 24-hour vet on hand.

Your vet will likely take blood samples, check your Italian Greyhound's gums and heart rate and may administer intravenous antibiotics and perhaps a catheter. Air in the stomach will be removed, either via a tube or needle. Abdominal surgery is almost always necessary.

c) Distichiasis

Distichiasis is an eyelash disorder found in dogs. Distichiasis is an eyelash that grows from an abnormal spot on the eyelid. The eyelash hair can come into contact with and damage the cornea or conjunctiva of the eye. It is most commonly seen in young dogs.

Symptoms

1) Few, if any, symptoms can be seen

2) Stiff eyelash

3) Pawing at eye

4) Abnormal tick or twitch of eyelid

5) Overflow of tears

6) Increased blood vessels in the cornea

7) Change in iris pigmentation

8) Corneal ulcers

Treatment

Removing the cause of irritation usually solves the problem. Treatment is not usually necessary. Continue to remove the eyelash that grows out and bothers the eye. If the hair is a frequent irritation to the eye, surgery may be required.

d) Demodex or Demodectic Mange

Some Italian Greyhounds can contract demodex or demodectic mange. Demodex is caused by tiny mites that feed on the hair follicles and glands of the skin. Demodex is considered to be less severe than sarcoptic mange. It is usually self-limiting. Once the mites are gone, the dog's immune system is usually able to keep them from returning. However, some Italian Greyhounds do not develop this immunity against the mites.

Symptoms

Demodectic mange may either be localized and affect specific areas of the body, or generalized, where it affects the entire body. If localized, symptoms are usually mild, with lesions occurring in patches, especially on the face, body, or legs. If generalized, symptoms will be more widespread and appear across the body. These symptoms include hair loss, a redness of the skin, and the appearance of scales and lesions.

Treatment

Localized demodex usually resolves itself. This happens in most cases. Generalized demodex, which is more severe, usually requires medication from your veterinarian.

e) Addison's Disease

The adrenal gland produces certain hormones that are necessary in the body. With Addison's Disease, or Hypoadrenocorticism, the adrenal gland does not make enough of the mineralocorticoids and glucocorticoids that the body needs.

Symptoms

1) Lethargy

2) Lack of appetite

3) Vomiting

4) Weight loss

5) Diarrhea

6) Shaking

7) Increased frequency of urination

8) Increased thirst

9) Depression

10) Dehydration

11) Weak pulse

12) Collapse

13) Low temperature

14) Blood in feces

15) Hair loss

16) Painful abdomen

Treatment

An acute episode of Addison's Disease is a veterinary emergency and will require immediate hospitalization for treatment. Treatment depends on the Italian Greyhound and severity of symptoms. Intravenous fluids may be necessary and it is usually necessary to replace deficient hormones. Hormone injections are standard for dogs that have been diagnosed.

f) Cushing's Disease

Cushing's Disease refers to Hyperadrenocorticism in dogs when it does not occur due to a benign pituitary gland tumor. It is a common endocrine disorder in dogs. When a disorder causes an excess of cortisone levels in the bloodstream, the metabolic process is hampered. This leads to gastrointestinal disorders and hypertension, among other bodily problems.

Symptoms

1) Increased thirst and urination (polydipsia and polyuria, respectively)

2) Increased hunger

3) Increased panting

4) Pot-bellied abdomen

5) Obesity

6) Fat pads on the neck and shoulders

7) Loss of hair

8) Lack of energy

9) Insomnia

10) Muscle weakness

11) Lack of a menstrual period

12) Shrinking of testicles

13) Darkening of the skin

14) Appearance of blackheads on the skin

15) Thin skin (from weight gain)

16) Bruising (from thin, weakened skin)

Treatment

Many Italian Greyhounds can be treated with drugs but the drugs can have side effects. Whether drugs can be used or not depends on the type of tumor and its location. Small, non-spreading tumors and small cancerous tumors can be surgically removed.

Chapter Ten: First Aid for Your Italian Greyhound

While it is important to work with your veterinarian, you should also be familiar with the basics of canine first aid. You can take several courses that will take you through more in-depth first aid but this section should get you started.

First Aid Kit

Every home that has an Italian Greyhound should have a first aid kit. Having a first aid kit will not only reduce the chance of having to go to the vet's office but will also give your dog precious minutes in a life-threatening situation. To create a first aid kit, fill an easy-to-access Tupperware or backpack with the following:

Important Numbers

Attach important numbers to your first-aid kit container so you never have to search for the number during a crisis. Numbers to have on hand are:

a) Your Veterinarian's Office

b) 24-hour Emergency Clinic - also have the address to the clinic

c) Canine Poison Control Centre

Medicine

There are a number of medications that you can have on hand, which will help you manage a condition or treat it quickly. Always keep track of expiration dates on the medication in your first aid kit.

a) Wound disinfectant for cuts

b) Sterile saline for washing out wounds

c) Antibiotic cream for cuts, scrapes, etc.

d) Cortisone cream for itchy skin

e) Ear cleaning solution

f) Eye wash solution

g) Antibiotic eye ointment

h) Hydrogen Peroxide for vomiting (only use at the discretion of your vet)

i) Activated Charcoal (only use at the discretion of your vet)

j) Gas X or any gas medication to help prevent bloat.

k) Anti-diarrheal medication

l) Benadryl for allergies (only use at the discretion of your vet)

Equipment

Sometimes having the right equipment can save the life of your Italian Greyhound, and it can also mean that it is treated at home and not at the vet clinic, reducing stress on everyone involved. Keep the following items on hand:

a) Magnifying glass

b) Nail clippers

c) Cotton balls

d) Cotton swabs

e) Cold packs

f) Heat packs

g) Thermometer

h) Towels and blankets in case of emergency transport

i) Scissors

k) Penlight

l) Styptic powder (to stop bleeding)

m) Nail clippers

n) Metal nail file

o) Oral syringe

p) Hemostat

q) KY Jelly

r) Eye Dropper

s) Tweezers

t) Disposable gloves

u) Bitter Apple (taste deterrent)

In addition to these items, you should have a crate or pet carrier near your first aid kit for transporting your Italian Greyhound.

Bandages and Other

Finally, make sure that you have bandages and a few odds and ends in your first aid kit. Things you should have are:

a) Karo Syrup

b) Vitacal or other nutritional supplement

c) Gatorade (for rehydration)

d) Band-Aids

e) Square Gauze

f) Non-stick pads

g) First aid tape

h) Bandage rolls

i) Vetwrap

Once you have all your supplies, place the kit in an easy to access area.

Dealing with an Emergency

Now that you have your first aid kit all ready for your Italian Greyhound, you are prepared for many of the little mishaps that life with a dog can bring. But are you ready for an emergency? Hopefully, the answer is yes. In this section we will go over some of the things you should know.

Here are some tips for dealing with an emergency.

1. Be Calm and Cautious

Although the first reaction is to panic, remain calm so your pup can sense your control of the situation. In addition, always be cautious when handling the dog in the midst of an emergency. If your Italian Greyhound is hurt or frightened, moving too roughly can injure it further or cause it to react.

2. Only Move Your Pup if Necessary

Make sure that you only move your Italian Greyhound if it needs to be moved. Sometimes lifting a dog too soon can compound an injury. If you can, wrap it carefully in a blanket and then move it.

3. Use your Voice

Italian Greyhounds often have a very strong bond with their owners and will react to your voice. If you talk to your pup in a loving and gentle manner, it will pick up on your tone and relax. This will make first aid or seeking medical help easier.

4. Keep your Italian Greyhound Warm

Wrap your Italian Greyhound in a warm towel or apply a warm compress if it is unconscious or showing any signs of going into shock. By keeping your pup warm, you are less likely to complicate its condition.

5. Staunch Blood Loss

In the event of an injury with blood loss, make a compression bandage or manually compress the area to prevent as much blood loss as possible. Remember that what you do in those first few minutes after a serious accident or emergency can mean the difference between life and death in some cases.

First Aid for Specific Conditions

i. Eye Injuries

When your Italian Greyhound has an eye injury, it is important to determine the type of injury. If there is something in the eye, carefully flush the eye with an eye-wash. You may need to have someone hold your pup's head while you put the liquid in the eye.

If your Italian Greyhound has injured its eye and it is bleeding, take an eye dropper and carefully rinse the eyeball. You do not want to flush but simply moisten it. Once it is moistened, apply a compress gently over the eye. This will help staunch the bleeding and will keep the eye free from exposure.

Seek immediate veterinary care after you have administered the first aid.

ii. Seizures

If your Italian Greyhound has a seizure you should contact your veterinarian as soon as possible. There can be several reasons for a seizure.

During the seizure, do not hold your Italian Greyhound. It can be very scared and disoriented during a seizure and may bite. In addition to staying clear, remove any objects that it might hurt itself on, such as furniture. Finally, turn off any type of stimulation. Lights should be turned off, radios as well, and people should try to stay quiet. While the seizure is happening, time it and write down when it started and when it ended. This is important in case there are recurring seizures.

After the seizure has stopped, comfort your pup. Wrap it in a warm blanket and then sit with it until it begins to act normally. Follow the directions of your vet and take your Italian Greyhound in for an examination.

iii. Heat Stroke

It is possible for Italian Greyhounds to develop heat stroke or heat exhaustion. To help prevent heat stroke, do not leave your dog outside when it is very hot. In addition, never leave a dog in a hot car.

If your Italian Greyhound does develop heat stroke, it is important to follow these steps:

1) Move the dog out of the hot area. Bring it to shade or inside.

2) Soak a towel with cold water.

3) Place the towel over the neck and head of your Italian Greyhound. Do not cover its eyes and keep its face clear of the fabric.

4) Repeat the process, wetting the towel down with cold water every few minutes.

5) If you cannot get to a vet, pour water over the dog's hind legs and abdomen.

6) While you are pouring water, massage the legs and then push the water off of the dog. Keeping the water moving will help cool the dog more.

As soon as you are able to, take your Italian Greyhound to the veterinarian. Heat exhaustion needs to be treated with the help of a trained professional.

iv. Fractures

Fractures are another emergency that will require veterinarian care. There is not a lot that you can do for your Italian Greyhound if there is a fracture. Do not attempt to create a splint; that can cause more harm than good.

Instead, take the time to muzzle your Italian Greyhound to keep it from biting. Then make a sling from a towel and blanket and keep it secure. Do not press on its chest or touch the area where the fracture is. Place a blanket over it to keep your dog warm, especially if it is going into shock.

Take your pet to the veterinarian's office immediately.

v. Burns

In the event of a burn, as long as it is not a severe burn that covers a large portion of your pup's body, you can treat it at home. If it is severe or covers a large area, seek medical attention immediately. For small burns, flush the burn area with large quantities of water until the burn starts to cool. You can use a burn relief ointment but make sure that it is not toxic if ingested.

vi. Choking

Choking can be a very scary situation for dog owners and it can happen very quickly. If your Italian Greyhound is choking, be sure to act quickly but be mindful that a choking dog is more likely to bite.

When a dog is choking, carefully grab its muzzle. Open its mouth and look inside it. If you can see the object that is causing the choking, take a pair of tweezers and carefully pull the object out. It is very important to be careful when you are doing this as it is easy to push the object further back into the throat. If you are unable to extract the object, seek medical help immediately.

If your Italian Greyhound stops breathing or collapses, place it on its side. Place your hand over the rib cage and firmly strike the rib cage three to four times with the flat of your palm. Repeat as necessary on your journey to the vet. While this may have no effect, administering this technique could force the air out of the lungs and force the obstruction out of your dog's throat.

vii. Shock

Another emergency that needs medical help, shock should be managed as you take your Italian Greyhound to the vet. Wrap your dog in a warm blanket and keep it warm. Also, lay it down and try to keep its head level with the rest of its body. Stay calm and comfort it to help minimize its discomfort.

viii. Bleeding

If your Italian Greyhound has an injury that has resulted in bleeding, it is important to staunch the flow of blood. Using a thick gauze pad, apply pressure to the wound. The pressure will aid in stimulating the clotting mechanism of blood.

If it is a minor injury, the bleeding will usually stop in a few minutes and you can then move to cleaning the wound. If it is severe, keep the pressure on the wound. Wrap your dog in a blanket or use a heat pad to keep it warm. This will help prevent shock as you seek veterinary care.

ix. Poisoning

Finally, if your Italian Greyhound is exposed to poison, it is important to immediately call poison control and/or your vet. They will guide you through the steps to take depending on the poison it has ingested. In the case of some toxins, you may be advised to administer active charcoal. In cases of consuming poisons, hydrogen peroxide may be recommended to induce vomiting.

If it is contact through skin or eyes, follow the directions on the container with the poison. Wash the area or flush it with water.

x. Administering CPR

CPR should only be used in the event that your Italian Greyhound is not breathing. If it is breathing, do not administer CPR or you could cause more harm than good.

With CPR, follow these steps:

1) Remain calm, and focus on your breathing.

2) Get someone to call your veterinarian.

3) Check the condition of your Italian Greyhound. Is it unconscious?

4) Open your dog's mouth and pull out its tongue until it is lying flat. Check to see if there is an obstruction. If there is, see the section on choking.

5) If there is not, close your Italian Greyhound's mouth and hold it closed. Place your mouth on its nose and breathe.

6) Watch the chest and breathe until it expands.

7) Pause and count to 5, then repeat with a breath.

8) Check your dog's heartbeat. The best place to do this is right above the pad on its front paw.

9) Lay your dog on its right side.

10) Slip your one hand under its right side in the lower half of its chest.

11) Place your hand, palm down over the lower half of its left side. This is where the heart is on a dog.

12) Press down about a half inch into the chest. (The depth varies with 1 inch for medium sized dogs, more for larger, less for smaller.)

13) Press down repeatedly, about 100 to 150 times per minute for small dogs, 80 to 120 times per minute for larger animals.

14) If you are using rescue breathing, have someone help you. One person can press the chest for 4 to 5 seconds for every single breath.

15) Repeat until you can feel a heartbeat or do it while someone else is driving you and your Italian Greyhound to the vet.

Although the information in this chapter will help you and your Italian Greyhound in an emergency, please remember that it should never replace the advice and care of a veterinarian.

Chapter Eleven: Spaying and Neutering

If you are not planning to breed your Italian Greyhound, one of the best health decisions you can make for your pet is to have them spayed or neutered. Having a female "spayed" means the ovaries and womb are surgically removed by your veterinary surgeon.

This procedure is very beneficial for female Italian Greyhounds and protects against a number of serious health conditions, since many of these conditions begin in the reproductive organs. Neutering of male Italian Greyhounds means the testicles are removed. This also has important benefits in health, behavior and the desire to stay close to home.

Many U.S. states and U.K. counties offer free or low-cost spaying/ neutering through vets. This makes this beneficial surgery affordable and easily accessible.

Benefits of Spaying Italian Greyhound Females

Disease Prevention

Early spaying helps prevent serious infections of the womb and breast cancer, which prove fatal in about 50% of cases in dogs. Spaying your pet before her first heat offers the best protection from these diseases and gives Italian Greyhounds a longer, healthier life.

Spayed females do not go into heat

A spayed female will not have the heat cycle that attracts unwanted attention from all the local male dogs.

Spaying Females Saves Money

The price of a pet's spaying surgery is far less than the cost of caring for an unexpected litter.

Benefits of Neutering Italian Greyhound Males

Disease Prevention

In addition to preventing unwanted litters, the neutering of male Italian Greyhounds prevents testicular cancer, if done before six months of age.

Male Italian Greyhounds stay close to home

An unneutered male will be completely obsessed with finding a mate. He will try to dig its way under fences and do everything possible to escape. Dogs that get free, risk serious injury from road traffic and fights with other males. Neutered dogs do not get lost so often, as they prefer to stay at home. Neutered dogs also rarely spray urine on your furnishings.

Neutering males saves money

In particular, neutering avoids the costs of testicular cancer treatment and vet fees for treating dog fight injuries from dogs competing for a mate.

Chapter Twelve: Breeding Your Italian Greyhound

Whether or not to breed your Italian Greyhound is an important decision that needs to be made before you purchase a puppy. Many puppies that make good, healthy pets are not registered as being suitable for breeding. Puppies registered as suitable for breeding when mature must have a bloodline that is completely free from genetic abnormalities. If you see breeding in your future, be sure to communicate this clearly to the breeder from whom you purchase your puppy.

Breeding an Italian Greyhound is a constant learning experience and it will help you to know someone who has years of experience. Try to maintain contact with the breeder of your puppy or get to know experts in an Italian Greyhound breed club.

Choosing the Right Dogs to Breed

The very first thing to do is to choose the right dogs, so ensure that you are familiar with the Italian Greyhound's breed standard.

If you are interested in breeding professionally, you may want to buy a good breeding pair – a male and a female Italian Greyhound. If you can only afford one dog, choose the best female dog from which to breed a litter. You can use stud dogs owned by other breeders, which is much more economical. If you have a good female Italian Greyhound, you will likely want to choose a different mate for her each time. That way you can see what kind of puppies she produces with different dogs and different bloodlines.

Serious dog breeders think in terms of generations. Having two or three different litter bloodlines from a bitch would give the best start for the future, if you retain one puppy from each litter for breeding. In general, when you are choosing a dog for breeding, you should bear the following points in mind:

Health

The Italian Greyhounds should be healthy and in good condition. They should be in proportionate weight for their build and also pass a health test from your vet. They should be free of disease so there is no risk of that disease being passed along to the young. If the vet voices any concerns over the health of the dogs, wait until they are in better health or choose different dogs.

Clearances

Clearances are very important to ensure the health of your puppies and the lifelong health of any dog you produce. Italian Greyhounds have several hereditary diseases, so the health tests you need are:

a) Eyes Certified by a board-certified ACVO

b) Ophthalmologist

c) OFA or PennHip certification for Hip Dysplasia

d) OFA evaluation for Autoimmune Thyroiditis

e) OFA evaluation for elbow dysplasia is optional in the breed.

In addition to these clearances, you should have the dogs tested for brucellosis, which is a sexually transmitted disease in dogs. Any dog that is being bred should be clear of this disease. Brucellosis can cause sterility in both males and females and can cause the mother (dam) to abort the puppies.

Registration

Before buying any dog for breeding, you should make sure the dog is registered with the kennel club you desire, or eligible to be registered.

Temperament

A good temperament is as important as health when it comes to breeding and it is a hereditary trait. If you have an Italian Greyhound that is nervous or prone to aggressive behavior it would not be a good idea to breed it.

Bloodlines

Another factor to take into account is the bloodline and how strong the pedigree is. When considering pedigrees for breeding, it is important to have a mentor or someone you trust give you some advice. You will need to study pedigrees as well as line-breeding, out-crossing and other breeding theories, which are not always easy to understand straightaway.

Age

Age is another crucial matter with dog breeding. Females should be no younger than 18 months of age for breeding and males should not be younger than 15 months of age. On the other hand, you should not breed a female after she is 7 years of age. Males can be bred for many years after that; however, the quality and quantity of sperm can be affected by age.

Ideally, males or females are not bred before they have had preliminary X-rays for hip dysplasia, so you can be reasonably sure they do not have this condition. Some health clearances cannot be done until the dog is older.

Physical Traits

Finally, you should choose dogs according to their physical traits. While the Italian Greyhounds you select must be good examples of the breed, you should also look at what each individual dog can bring to their future puppies. For instance, if both dogs have excellent ears according to the breed standard, the odds are very high that the puppies will inherit those ears. A good coat on a female may be passed on to the puppies, even if the male has a coat that is not as good. A good body shape on the male may be passed on to the puppies and so on. Choosing complementary traits will improve your puppies and your bloodlines, too.

The Italian Greyhound Breeding Community

While many people enjoy exhibiting their dogs at shows, it is not a necessity for dog breeders. However, showing your dogs, or merely attending shows, does have many benefits for dog breeders.

Participation in these events puts you in touch with a community of reputable breeders and allows you to see many different Italian Greyhounds and compare traits. It also keeps you informed about news in your breeder community and has definite advantages for anyone interested in breeding dogs.

Breeding Responsibilities

Before you make the final decision about which dogs to breed, take a moment to remember that breeding is a significant responsibility. There is often very little money to be earned when doing it properly and it is a full-time commitment.

While the mother (dam) will help with the care, there is a lot to be done during the first 8 weeks (or more) when you are raising puppies at home. In addition, breeders need to be prepared to accept any puppies that are returned for some reason.

Breeding is not for the faint of heart, but one thing is certain: holding a tiny, newborn Italian Greyhound in your hands is worth all the work, money and commitment.

Vaccinations

Before breeding your female Italian Greyhound, make sure she is up-to-date on her vaccinations. Mothers pass temporary immunity to their puppies at birth, protecting them against common dog diseases. Therefore, try to ensure females being prepared to breed have maximum levels of immunity.

In the UK and Europe, it is also recommended that bitches receive the canine herpes virus vaccination before breeding. Canine herpes virus is extremely widespread, affecting up to 90 percent of all dogs. It is harmless to most adult dogs, but it can sometimes kill newborn puppies. The vaccine is very helpful in protecting newborns. Unfortunately, this vaccine is not yet available in the United States.

Heat Cycle

When a female dog reaches sexual maturity, she will begin what is known as a heat or in season. A heat or heat cycle is when the female begins bleeding and will be ready to accept the male within a few days.

For Italian Greyhounds, the first heat usually occurs between six months and a year. However, a bitch should never be bred on her first heat or before the age of 18 months to 2 years. Some females take longer to have their first heat than others. It is not uncommon for an Italian Greyhound to be closer to 12 months or even up to 2 years, before she has her first heat.

The average interval between heat cycles and coming in season is roughly six months, but there is some variation in frequency. Some Italian Greyhounds come into season every four months and some just once a year.

The signs of being in season

With heat cycles, there are signs of the heat cycle before the discharge begins. Often the vulva begins to swell and the female will begin licking her back end and vulva more. In addition, she may be urinating more frequently and if you have any male dogs in the home, you may notice them paying more attention to her than usual. The female will begin to have a bloody discharge and this can vary in quantity between females and even between heat cycles. Some females have very little discharge and others have a lot. The bleeding should not last more than 3 weeks and should become paler in color after the first few days. The dog can get pregnant only during the first 2 to 3 days after the heat cycle has started.

Stages of Heat Cycle

When the dog has the heat cycle, she is also in season. The heat cycle has 3 main stages:

Proestrus

When your bitch is in the first stage of her heat cycle, she will reject male dogs.

Oestrus

The oestrus starts from Day 4 and may last a few days to weeks. During the oestrus period, bitches are ready to mate and will accept male dogs.

Diestrus

Diestrus is the final part of the heat cycle, lasting between 4 and 14 days, depending on the length of the heat cycle and how long the oestrus lasts. During this time, the dog will bleed less and will not want to mate.

Natural or Artificial?

When you are breeding, you can choose between allowing the dogs to breed naturally or by using A.I. (Artificial Insemination).

Natural breeding is when you allow the male dog to mount the female and achieve a tie. This is more often the preferred way to breed. Many breeders learn how to do artificial inseminations themselves.

However, if you use frozen sperm, you need to have the A.I. done by a specialized, reproductive veterinarian. Frozen sperm is often shipped by one breeder to another over vast distances, at considerable expense. Therefore, it is more cost-efficient to employ a professional to ensure the insemination does not fail. With A.I., the sperm is delivered to the cervix through a sterilized tube inserted into the vagina.

There are several reasons why you would use A.I. and these are:

1) The chosen stud dog lives too far away.

2) A dominant female will not allow a male to mount.

3) A sexually inexperienced stud dog.

4) A persistent hymen in the bitch.

5) Size incompatibility.

A.I. is less likely to spread an S.T.D., but it usually produces smaller litter sizes. Also, it is important to properly judge when ovulation occurs, which can be difficult and is usually done with progesterone testing by your vet. Many breeders use A.I. with fresh semen, even when the stud dog is on the premises. This is done to avoid any injury to the stud dog and to avoid any chance of passing disease.

When to Breed

You have the stud dog, a bitch in heat and you have made the decision to go with a natural tie. This means you are ready to start breeding soon - but maybe not right away.

Breeding times differs from female to female, but if you have the male in your home, you can begin breeding as soon as the female starts accepting him. Allow them to mate only every other day. This gives the sperm time to recover in numbers and you will get a better sperm count for each mating.

Progesterone testing

If you do not have a male, you can do progesterone testing to try to narrow down when your female is most fertile. Progesterone testing is done with a blood test, but you can also do a vaginal smear, although this is not as accurate.

When using progesterone testing, follow the guidelines of your veterinarian. Testing your bitch is an excellent way to identify if she is ready to be bred. In addition, you can also pinpoint the best mating time by observing her behavior.

A female that is ready to be bred will exhibit the following:

1) Vaginal discharge will turn to a light pink or straw color.

2) The female will back up into the male.

3) She will hold her tail to the side (known as flagging).

4) She will be playful with the male.

5) She will stand still when the male is sniffing her.

6) She will not attack the male when he tries to mount her.

When you see these signs, your female is ready to be bred. Even with these signs, however, progesterone testing can be more accurate for determining the exact right time for mating to result in a pregnancy.

48 hours before ovulation

There is a spike in the LH (luteinizing hormone) 48 hours prior to ovulation, when the egg is ready to be fertilized. This spike will trigger the progesterone levels to begin rising, signaling the best times for breeding. For example, after the LH surge and the rise in progesterone, carry out a natural breeding three days later. The sperm in fresh semen can survive 5 to 7 days in the female dog's uterus.

When to do the A.I. (chilled or frozen sperm)

Artificial insemination using fresh, chilled semen can be used 4 days after the rise in progesterone. Sperm in chilled semen survive 48 to 72 hours after insemination.

Artificial insemination using frozen semen can be used 5 days after the progesterone surge. Sperm in frozen semen only survives 24 hours once it has been deposited in the uterus by insemination.

The Act of Mating

When your female is ready to be bred, it is time to let the dogs be together. Never leave them unattended as injuries can occur if the female attacks the male or she becomes scared.

The stud dog will spend some time sniffing the rear of the female and he may begin to lick the vulva. The female will stand still and move her tail out of the way. She will also back into the male.

If you have a maiden bitch or an inexperienced stud dog, you can have success without intervening, but things often go much better if you are on hand to assist. For example, inexperienced stud dogs can sometimes be so excited they will mount the wrong end of the female.

Positioning the female

If you have invested money in a high stud fee or driven a long way to arrange a mating, you or the stud dog owner may decide to lend a hand. For instance, you can hold the bitch in position or guide the male in the right direction. However, if you have an experienced bitch and/or stud dog, the process is smoother and quicker, when the time is right

As the male builds excitement, he will mount the female, wrapping his front legs around the hips of the female. He will begin to thrust against the female and his penis will enter the vulva. During this action, the bright-red glans penis will come out of the sheath. The penis will extend into the vulva until the dog locks with the female.

Once the lock happens, the male and female cannot be separated. Do not try to separate them as you can hurt both the male and the female. Once locked (or "tied"), the male will lift his leg over the rear of the female and then turn so they are standing with their back ends together. The penis will bend, but still be inserted in the vulva. Dogs remain locked for 10 - 30 minutes until the penis loses some of its swelling and is released from the lock/tie.

Myths about becoming pregnant

One myth holds that a female cannot get pregnant if there is no lock/tie. This is not true. When the dog is thrusting, sperm is released. The fluid that is released when they are locked is very low in sperm and is a lubricant used to push the sperm through the cervix.

Signs of Pregnancy

During the initial stages of pregnancy, it can be difficult to determine whether or not a bitch is pregnant because a female dog goes through the same hormone changes whether she is pregnant or not. In fact, even a female that has not been mated can present the symptoms of pregnancy. This can be a suspenseful time for a breeder, when they wonder whether a mating has been successful. The female may have morning sickness and a decreased appetite for food, but some females are not affected in this way at all.

After the first 30 days, a pregnant dog will begin to show some symptoms including:

a) Nipple growth

b) Darkening of the nipples

c) Decreased appetite early on

d) Increased appetite around week 6

e) Clinginess and other behavior changes

f) Pear shape of the abdomen

g) Weight gain

Ultrasound Test

At 30 to 35 days, you can have an ultrasound done to confirm pregnancy. At this early stage it is not possible to tell how many puppies there are.

The gestational period for Italian Greyhounds is between 63 to 65 days after the time of first mating. However, this varies depending on the individual dog. If you have used progesterone testing, whelping is normally exactly 63 days after ovulation. Even if you have bred your dog late in the heat, you can still count on 63 days from ovulation rather than from the date of mating.

Experienced vets and breeders can palpate a bitch's abdomen and feel the puppies. At 30 days, puppies are about the size of walnuts. After this time they cannot be felt again for several weeks.

X-ray at 45 days gestation

After 45 days gestation, an X-ray can be done and the puppies can be counted. Sometimes counts are wrong, as puppies may be covered by their siblings. However, it is important to know how many puppies there are, so at whelping you know when all of the pups have been safely born.

Feeding during pregnancy

During pregnancy, continue to feed your female her normal dog food for the first six weeks. After this time, you should begin to increase her food, as she needs extra calories to help the pups develop. Breeders will change to a highly nutritious diet with more calories and sometimes feed pregnant bitches on puppy food to get the balance right. You can add some prenatal vitamins for dogs to her diet but do not add any additional calcium or other supplements at this time.

Once the puppies are born, feed the mother as much as she wants to eat, especially if she has several puppies. She will need the extra calories to produce milk.

Whelping

The time for whelping the puppies is drawing closer. This is an exciting time, but it is also a busy time for you. It is very important to have all your supplies ready and to begin preparing for the puppies a few weeks before their arrival.

Whelping supplies

The main priority is to have the whelping supplies on hand. These are essential for helping your puppies and mother. If the birthing goes well, you will need to intervene very little with the labor. In the worst case, you could have to rush your pregnant Italian Greyhound to the vet clinic for an emergency section. Even an easy whelping can result in puppies in distress, so it is important to have the equipment on hand to help the puppies.

Whelping Box: This should be a clean, square box in which the mother can birth and raise her puppies. You can make the box yourself or purchase a whelping box.

The box needs to be sturdy and of good quality as it will be the puppies' home for the next few weeks.

Blankets: Have a lot of clean blankets on hand for your whelping box. Labor is messy and you have to change the bedding in the whelping box several times during labor.

Newspaper: In addition to blankets, have a large amount of newspaper to put down during the whelping process. You can sometimes obtain end-rolls from your local newspaper provider. These are plain paper rolls, without the ink, so they will be much cleaner than using newspapers.

Basket: A cloth-lined laundry basket or large plastic container to put the puppies in when the female is birthing another puppy.

Hot water bottles: Towel-wrapped hot water bottles are needed for the basket to keep the puppies warm when they are not with their mother. Puppies will cuddle up to the hot water bottles if they are feeling cold and move away if they are too warm. You can also use a heating pad, but wrap it with a towel so the puppies do not get burned.

Scales: Have a kitchen scale so you can properly weigh each puppy as it is born. This is a tool you will need throughout the time the litter is with you, to weigh the puppies regularly.

Notebook and pens: Create a notebook that charts the progress of each individual puppy. Start with the puppy's sex, identifier, date of birth, presentation at birth, time born, color/pattern and weight. This will help you keep track of each puppy's health and progress.

Identifier: This can be yarn, puppy collars, or nail polish for their nails. Basically, it is anything you can use safely to identify each puppy. Use the same color for that puppy throughout the 8 weeks that you have the puppies.

In addition to those items, have the following items available in a kit. Be sure to sterilize all of the instruments, especially the scissors and hemostatic clamps:

a) Sharp scissors

b) Hemostatic clamp

c) Surgical gloves

d) Iodine swabs

e) Alcohol swabs

f) Lubricating jelly such as K-Y

g) Digital thermometer

h) Vaseline

i) Nursing bottles for puppies

j) Liquid puppy vitamins

k) Puppy formula

l) Energizing glucose drops

m) Bulb syringe

Place all of the items into a clean and easy to access container close to the whelping box.

Stages of Labor

Before Labor

The gestation period for dogs is about 63 days. However, it is important to monitor your Italian Greyhound during the days leading up to the delivery.

Around day 56 to 58, the female should start searching for a nesting site. Encourage her to nest in the whelping box by sitting next to it and calmly petting her. Do not discourage her scratching at the bedding, as this is normal.

In addition, you should start taking her temperature about a week before her due date. The average temperature of your female will be between 99ºF to 101°F (37.22ºC to 38.33°C). Mark down her temperature each day and, closer to the due date, start checking her temperature several times each day.

About 48 hours before labor, her temperature will have a spike up to about 101.5°F (38.6°C) or higher. Within 24 hours after that, the temperature will drop. Once it drops below 98°F (36.7°C), you will have between 12 to 24 hours before the litter is expected.

First Stage of Labor

After the final temperature drop, you will start to notice a number of signs that indicate your female is going into labor.

For about 2 to 12 hours, your female will become restless. She may start to nest even more than she did before, or she may become very stressed, wanting to wander around the house. You may see some shivering and she will probably be changing her position frequently. Her eyes will dilate and she will watch you and want to be with you. Try to stay near the whelping box so she can settle in.

She may lose her appetite and it is not uncommon for bitches to vomit at this time. She may also try to defecate and not be able to. This is caused by the pressure building up in her stomach. If you take your Italian Greyhound outside to eliminate, keep her on a leash and check the spot where she squatted. It is not uncommon for puppies to be born outside. Finally, you may see some mucus being discharged from the vulva.

Second Stage of Labor

During the second stage of labor, your female should start rearranging her bedding even more. You will also notice her looking at her back end more frequently and she may start licking her vulva. Shivering is more noticeable and she will have episodes where she is panting heavily. You may be able to see mild contractions going across her belly or you may feel a tightening of her abdomen.

Again, your Italian Greyhound may vomit and she may ask to go outside more frequently. Remember to stay with her when she eliminates to make sure a puppy is not born outside.

Note: At this time, if the discharge turns to a dark green color, seek medical help. Dark green discharge is only normal after a puppy is born. If it appears before, it can indicate a life-threatening problem for both your bitch and her litter.

Third Stage of Labor

Ensure the room is warm, quiet and calm. This is the stage of labor when the puppies begin to be expelled or whelped. During this time, the contractions will become stronger and you will be able to see them. They will also occur closer together.

Your Italian Greyhound female may vomit during this time and you will notice that she begins pushing and grunting. Some bitches prefer to squat when they have their puppies, others lie down on their side. Let the female decide how she is going to birth the puppies. As she is pushing, you will see a membrane sac filled with clear fluid containing a puppy come out of the vulva. Puppies are born in their own sac and it may burst while being delivered or as the female breaks it.

Breech births

Puppies are born both front feet first and breech, with their tail or back feet presented first. Each puppy is followed by the afterbirth. Females often eat the afterbirth which contains hormones to stimulate milk production.

After a puppy is born be sure to count each placenta, to make sure every single one is expelled. A retained placenta or "afterbirth" can cause a serious infection and lead to complications for your female. Puppies are usually born in quick successions of two or three at a time after which you may have to wait an hour or so before the next puppies are born. The process of birthing can last up to 24 hours, depending on the size of the litter.

Weigh and identify the pups

In between the birthing of puppies, weigh the latest puppies to be born, jot down all the notes on each one and place an identification yarn on every puppy.

Problems to Watch For

Watching a litter being born is a very exciting thing but make sure you are prepared for any problems.

a) If the female is pushing for longer than 30 minutes without expelling a puppy, contact and follow the advice of your veterinarian. It could mean a puppy is trapped blocking the birth canal.

b) If there is a long period of time between puppy births, contact your veterinarian, especially if you are expecting more puppies.

c) When the puppies are born, allow them to nurse from their mother between births.

d) Every time she is ready to push, remove the puppies to your basket. This keeps her from being distracted by the puppies and she is less likely to sit on a puppy or hurt it.

e) Try to let her do the work herself. If you get too involved, you could cause her to stop laboring. Only get involved if she looks like she needs help.

Eclampsia

When the bitch's milk starts to flow during whelping, watch out for the effects of eclampsia, which can cause her to experience contractions that convulse the whole body. This can limit her movement and interfere with the birthing of the pups. The problem is that the demand for calcium is suddenly increased and the parathyroid gland is sometimes unable to respond quickly enough for her needs to be fully met.

If your female becomes fatigued during delivery or seems to have run out of steam, you can give her some vanilla ice cream for energy. After whelping, be sure she eats something light but nutritious and has plenty of fresh water. You can offer her some chicken or broth if she seems to have lost her appetite. She should soon be feeling hungry after nursing the litter of puppies.

The Weeks after Whelping

It is also important to note that in the weeks after giving birth, the gland that regulates the parathyroid hormone (which governs the amount of calcium stored within the mother), can become depleted. Once diagnosed with eclampsia, the new mother will be prescribed calcium supplements by your vet. In addition, calcium-rich foods such as cottage cheese and goat's milk will also help her to recover after giving birth.

Puppy Care and Development Tasks

Raising pups is a fun activity and, for the first few weeks, the mother does the majority of the work. She will clean the puppies and feed them. However, it does not mean that you have nothing to do - you will be very busy with your own chores. Below is a chart of what you need to do with the puppies while they are growing.

Week 1

The puppies sleep the majority of the time. When they are awake, they will crawl towards warmth and milk. The puppies have their eyes and ears closed and are helpless at this age.

a) Chart weight twice a day.

b) Trim nails at the end of the week.

c) Handle the puppies daily to check their health and start neurological stimulation.

d) Clean the bedding daily.

e) Monitor the mother and her health.

f) Keep the whelping box temperature about 85°F (29.4°C).

Week 2

Puppies are beginning to move around more and they are awake for longer periods.

a) Trim nails at the end of the week.

b) Hold the puppies in different positions to accustom them to being handled.

c) Monitor the mother and her health.

d) Clean bedding daily.

e) Weigh puppies once a day.

Eyes and ears

Eyes will begin to open at 8 - 10 days and ears will open near the end of week 2 or the start of week 3.

Week 3

Eyes and ears will be open by the end of this week and the pups will be more active. They will start trying to walk and go to the bathroom without stimulation from mother. They will begin to play and their little teeth will be starting to show.

a) Continue to handle the puppies.

b) Trim nails at end of the week.

c) Begin getting the pups familiar with items such as grooming brushes and combs.

d) Weigh puppies every other day.

e) Monitor the mother and her health.

f) Begin weaning process.

g) Start with milk replacer once a day for two days.

h) Then add a mushy food once per day.

i) Clean bedding daily.

Week 4

During this week, the puppies will be more playful and begin growling. They will also be eating mushy food and nurse occasionally.

Their mother will be resting more and feeding less, but should still be with them a lot. As soon as they start eating foods other than their mother's milk, cleaning up dog mess will be your job.

a) Continue to handle the puppies.

b) Trim nails at end of the week.

c) Begin familiarizing the puppies to other things such as noises and other animals in your home.

d) Weigh puppies every other day.

e) Monitor the mother and her health.

f) Shift the food to be the consistency of porridge and add one extra meal a day.

g) Clean bedding daily.

Week 5

Puppies are more alert and they will be active. You will start to see temperament emerging, and may even see sexual play. Puppies grow quickly during this time.

a) Weigh puppies two to three times each week.

b) Reduce the mother's diet to stop her milk production.

c) Start reducing the amount of liquid in the puppies' food.

d) Continue to handle the puppies.

e) Trim nails at end of the week.

f) Continue getting the puppies accustomed to a range of stimuli.

g) Clean bedding daily.

Week 6

Puppies are developing quickly and showing signs of their own personalities. Mother will spend less time with the puppies at this stage.

a) Give each puppy time alone.

b) Weigh the puppies weekly.

c) Continue reducing the amount of liquid in the puppies' food.

d) Continue to handle the puppies.

e) Trim nails at end of the week.

f) Continue widening the puppies' range of stimuli.

g) Clean bedding daily.

Week 7

Puppies will be able to hear and see fully at this stage. They will be very inquisitive and can get into some problems if you just take your eyes off them for a second.

a) Give each puppy time alone.

b) Weigh the puppies weekly.

c) Puppies should be fully weaned and on puppy food.

d) Continue to handle the puppies.

e) Trim nails at end of the week.

f) Continue socializing the puppies to a range of stimuli.

g) Clean bedding daily.

Week 8

Puppies are at the age where they can start going to their new homes. This is the week when a fear period can occur so make sure you do not stress them too much.

a) Give each puppy some time alone.

b) Weigh the puppies weekly.

c) Trim nails at end of the week.

d) Continue socializing the puppies to a range of stimuli.

e) Clean bedding daily.

f) Start training puppies that have not already left for their new home.

As you can see, raising a litter of puppies is a lot of work. It is advisable to have homes lined up for the puppies before you breed, or at least to know how you will place your puppies.

Italian Greyhound puppies may be highly desirable, but it is still necessary to let people know you are breeding a litter. You will want to make sure your puppies are going to good homes after you have put so much work into breeding the litter and raising them. Most breeders have a waiting list and take deposits on their puppies when they are born.

Chapter Thirteen: Resources

Here are some resources that will further help you in making ownership of your Italian Greyhound more fulfilling and easier.

Owner Resources

It is important to note that we are not affiliated with any of these sites. Always discuss your dog's health and training issues with trained professionals.

AltVetMed: http://www.altvetmed.org/

Association of Professional Dog Trainers: APDT.com

American College of Veterinary Nutrition: http://www.acvn.org/

American Dog Trainers Network: http://www.inch.com/~dogs/

Breeder.net: http://www.breeders.net/

Behavior Adjustment Training: www.empoweredanimals.com

Canine Eye Registration Foundation: http://web.vmdb.org/home/CERF.aspx

Canine Health Foundation: http://www.akcchf.org/

DogAware: http://dogaware.com/

Canine Health Information Center: http://www.caninehealthinfo.org/

Certification Council for Professional Dog Trainers: http://www.ccpdt.org

David Mech (Recantation of Dominance Theory): http://www.davemech.org/news.html

Dog Food Advisor: www.dogfoodadvisor.com

DogAware: http://dogaware.com/

DogFood.guru

Dog Owners' Guide: http://www.canismajor.com/

Dog Time: http://dogtime.com/

Dr. Jean Dodds Vaccination Protocol: http://www.weim.net/emberweims/Vaccine.html

Dr. Foster and Smith Pet Education: http://www.peteducation.com/

Dr Sophia Yin (Further debunking of dominance and pack theories): http://drsophiayin.com/philosophy/dominance

Healthy Pet: http://www.aaha.org/pet_owner/

International Association of Animal Behavior Consultants: https://iaabc.org

Medline Plus: http://www.nlm.nih.gov/medlineplus/pethealth.html

Orthopedic Foundation for Animals: http://www.offa.org/

PAW: http://www.paw-rescue.org/

Pet Diets: https://www.petdiets.com/

Pet Loss: http://www.petloss.com/

Pet-Loss Support: http://www.pet-loss.net/

PetMD: http://www.petmd.com/

Pet Pharmacy: http://www.veterinarypartner.com

Pet Professional Guild: http://www.petprofessionalguild.com

Petstyle: http://www.petstyle.com/

Rainbow Bridge Pet Loss: https://rainbowsbridge.com/

Suzanne Clothier, Myth of Reinforcing Fear:

http://fearfuldogs.com/myth-of-reinforcing-fear/

Terrific Pets: http://www.terrificpets.com/

VetInfo: http://www.vetinfo.com/

Vetmedicine: http://vetmedicine.about.com/

Vetquest: http://www.vetquest.com/

Whole Pet: http://www.wholepetvet.com/

Resource for dog nutrition and food: Dog Food Logic by Linda Case

CPSIA information can be obtained
at www.ICGtesting.com
Printed in the USA
LVOW10s1805180118
563133LV00019B/968/P